A to Z 神秘案件 中英双语
第一辑

THE CANARY CAPER
金丝雀之谜

[美] 罗恩·罗伊 著
[美] 约翰·史蒂文·格尼 绘　高琼 译

湖南少年儿童出版社　小博集
·长沙·

人物介绍

三人小组的成员，聪明勇敢，喜欢读推理小说，紧急关头总能保持头脑冷静。喜欢在做事之前好好思考！

丁丁

三人小组的成员，活泼机智，喜欢吃好吃的食物，常常有意想不到的点子。

乔希

三人小组的成员，活泼开朗，喜欢从头到脚穿同一种颜色的衣服，总是那个能找到大部分线索的人。

露丝

丢失的金丝雀莫扎特的主人，住在林荫街，她最先发现自己的宠物不见了。

戴维斯太太

丢失的兔子维奥莱特的主人，住在野鸡巷3号。

帕杜医生

丢失的鹦鹉的主人，住在蓟花街。

格温先生

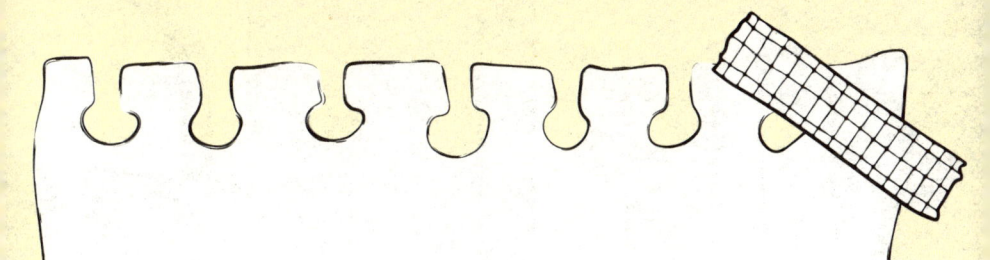

字母 C 代表 confusion，疑惑不解……

"现在，我们当中必须有一个人跑到警察局去。"丁丁说。

…………

突然，有三件事情同时发生了：楼上的灯亮了，丁丁听见有人在大声尖叫，敞开的窗户里传出了响亮刺耳的警哨声。

丁丁跳了起来，不知道该怎么办。戴维斯太太在楼上，窃贼很可能跟她待在同一个房间里！

可是，尖叫声是谁发出来的呢？

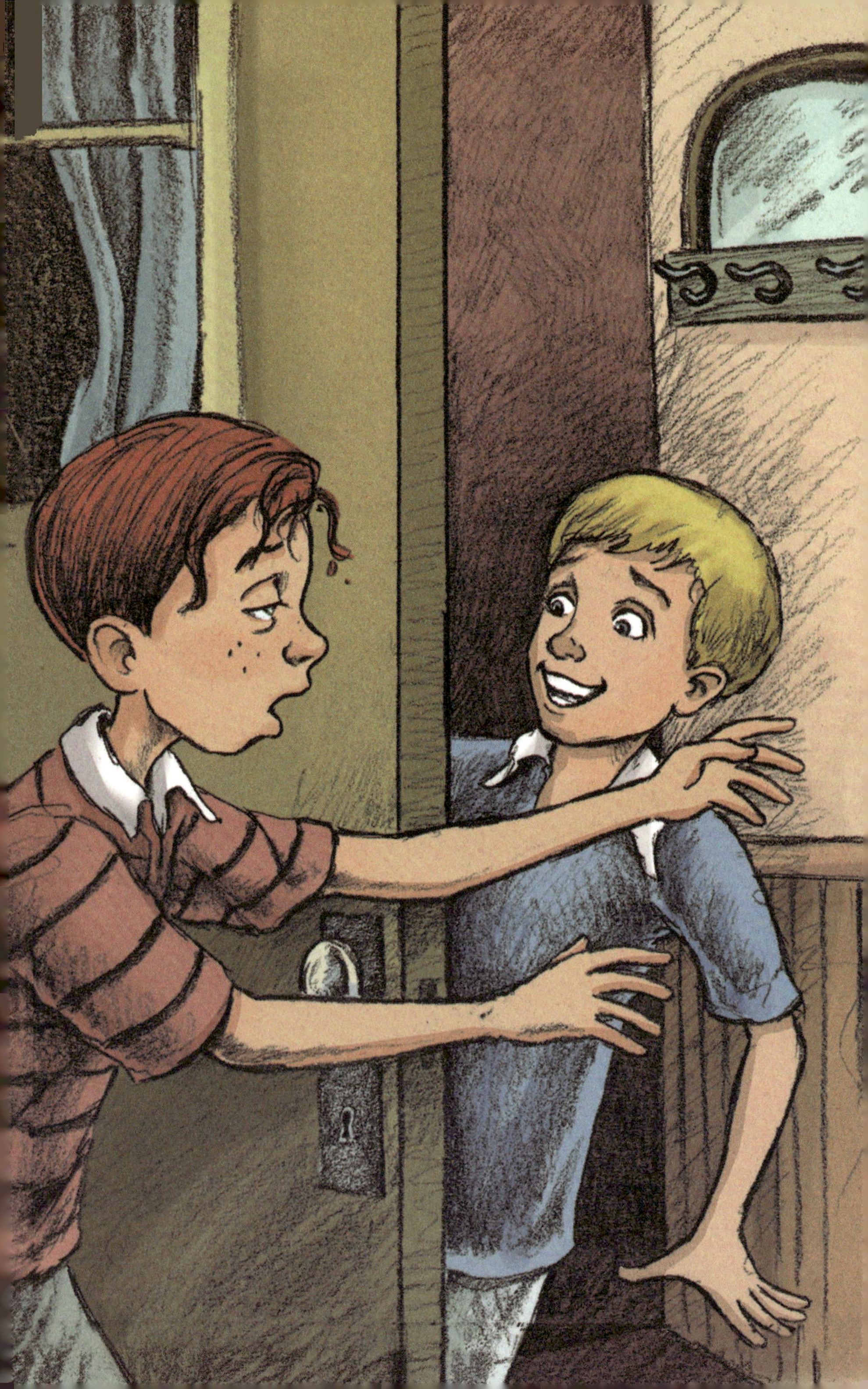

第一章

丁丁·邓肯打开正门,看见他最要好的朋友乔希·平托站在台阶上。"嘿,乔希,快进来吧!"丁丁跟他打招呼,"我刚刚吃完午餐呢。"

乔希擦着前额上的汗水,从丁丁身旁匆匆进了屋。"我们绝对是选了夏天最热的一天去看马戏团表演。"他说,"我刚刚洗完澡,但还是感觉很热。"

丁丁咧着嘴笑道:"你洗过澡了吗?我们来想

9

想，这个月你洗了两次澡，对吧？"

"哈哈哈，太好笑了。"乔希说着，打开冰箱门，撩起他的衬衫，"啊哈，这样好爽啊！"

"要是让我妈妈逮到，你就不会觉得爽了。"丁丁说。

乔希一把拿起苹果汁，扑通一声坐到椅子上。"你太搞笑了，不过天气太热，我都笑不出来了。"他说着，给自己倒了一杯苹果汁，"露丝在哪儿呢？差不多到出发时间了"。

"她正在隔壁自己家里等着呢。"丁丁一边说，一边把自己的盘子放进水槽，"我得赶紧去楼上去刷牙了。"

"别刷牙了——马戏团表演在等着我们呢！"

丁丁一边咧着嘴笑，一边指着操作台上一个小丑样子的饼干罐："拿块饼干吃吧。我马上就下来。"

乔希径直奔向饼干罐，说道："慢慢地刷你的牙吧，不着急。"

"别吃光了！"丁丁一边说，一边三步并作两步地上楼去了。

"丁丁,"他妈妈喊道,"是你在家里跑吗?"

"不好意思,妈妈,"他回应道,"我们赶时间呢。马戏团的门票周四半价,我们得赶在一点钟之前到那里。"

丁丁刷好牙,用梳子梳了梳金色的头发,冲下了楼。

"唐纳德·戴维·邓肯!"他妈妈大声喊道,"不许在屋子里乱跑!"

突然,厨房里的电话响了。

"知道了,妈妈!"丁丁一边回应着,一边抓起电话,他看见乔希正把一整块饼干塞进嘴里,"你好,这里是邓肯家。"

丁丁听完电话对面的请求,说:"我们五分钟之后就过来。"随即他挂断了电话。

"我们五分钟之后去哪里?"乔希问道。

"去戴维斯太太家里。你知道她的金丝雀莫扎特吗?它逃走了。"

"那马戏团表演怎么办?"乔希问道,"门票半价呢,你不会忘了吧?"

丁丁耸了耸肩:"这样的话,我们只能买全价票去看了。戴维斯太太需要我们去帮她。"

他们两个来到隔壁露丝的家门前，按响门铃。来开门的是四岁的纳特·哈撒韦，只见他抬起头，用两只大大的蓝眼睛盯着丁丁。

"嘿，纳特，"丁丁跟他打招呼，"露丝准备好了吗？"

纳特的嘴上、脸上、T恤衫上全都是巧克力，手里还抱着一个破破烂烂的恐龙玩偶。

"她——要果士。"纳特嘴里塞满了巧克力，含糊不清地说道。

丁丁不禁笑出了声："她怎么了？"

这时，露丝突然从纳特身后冒了出来。

"妈妈，我们现在出发了！"她朝屋子里大声喊了一句。

乔希用双手捂住自己的耳朵："露丝，你应该去做汽车销售员。这样你就可以整天大声叫嚷，还能以此赚钱了。"

露丝走到屋子外面，关上了门。"我将来是要当总统的，这个你再清楚不过了。"她甜甜地说,"而且我就算做销售,也是个女销售员[1],乔希。"

露丝喜欢全身穿同一种颜色的衣服。她今天的装扮是紫色的——从脚上的运动鞋到头上束着黑色鬈发的束发带,全都是紫色的。

他们沿着林荫街往前走,趁着这段时间,丁丁把戴维斯太太丢失金丝雀的事情告诉了露丝。

"莫扎特从鸟笼里飞出去了?"露丝说,"真希望它不会飞到这儿来。泰格一口就能把一只金丝雀吞下肚子。"

"你家那只肥猫一口能吞下一只火鸡。"乔希说。

露丝翻了个白眼。"泰格只是丰满,"她纠正道,"才不肥。我们来比赛吧,看谁跑得快!"

他们到达目的地的时候,戴维斯太太正站在自家黄色大房子的门口。"谢谢你们及时赶过来。"她说。

---

1. 英语里男、女销售员的拼写不同,所以乔希说露丝应该做"销售员(salesman)"时,露丝说自己就算做销售,也是个"女销售员(saleswoman)"。——编者

戴维斯太太手里拿着手帕,两只眼睛通红:"我都不知道还能给谁打电话了。"

"没关系的。"丁丁说,"莫扎特到底怎么了?"

"吃过早餐,我把鸟笼挂在屋子后面让它呼吸新鲜空气。可是,等我去给它送午餐的时候,鸟笼里竟然空空如也!"

"我敢肯定它就在附近的某个地方。别担心!"丁丁安慰她道。

丁丁、乔希和露丝跑到后院去,只见莫扎特的鸟笼正挂在一棵苹果树上。

"我们分头行动吧,"丁丁说道,"把树丛和花圃全都找一遍。"

孩子们到处都找过了,没有放过一棵树、一丛灌木、一个花圃。戴维斯太太在屋子后面的门廊上看着孩子们寻找。"有什么发现吗?"她问丁丁。

丁丁摇了摇头:"没有,不过我们会继续找的。"

"今天天气多好啊!"戴维斯太太说,"希望没有打乱你们几个的计划。"

"等找到莫扎特,我们就去看马戏团表演。"

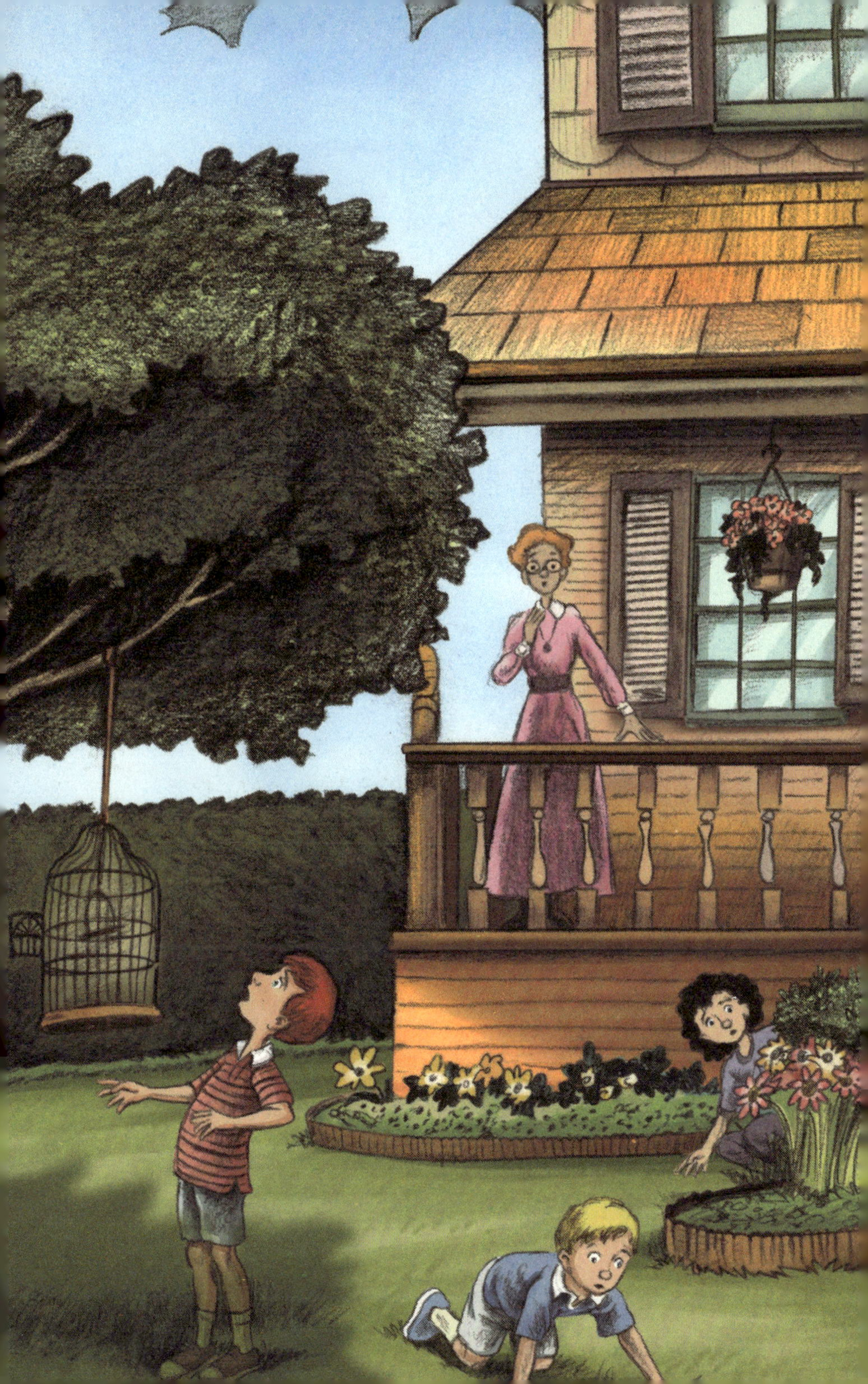

丁丁告诉她。

"马戏团表演!哎呀,不要因为我的事情让你们的计划泡汤了!"戴维斯太太说,"莫扎特知道自己的鸟笼在这里。我敢肯定,它很快就会飞回家的。"

不过,丁丁看得出来,戴维斯太太并不是真的那么肯定。"好吧,不过随后我们会给您打电话的。"他承诺道。

于是他们跟戴维斯太太道过别,朝着高中走去。昨天,廷克镇流动马戏团刚在学校棒球场布置完,周一晚上就要离开了。

孩子们穿过一辆辆马戏团的拖车和卡车,向入场大门走去。拖车的两侧用油漆画了小丑、老虎和大象的图案。

他们到达的时间是一点零五分,不过女售票员还是让他们买半价票进去了,他们每个人花了一美元。

"我们首先要做什么呢?"露丝问道。

"先吃饭吧。"乔希说。

"不行,"丁丁说,"你已经吃过午餐了。你刚才一阵狼吞虎咽，很可能把我妈妈的一半饼干都给吃了。我们先转转，看看这里都有些什么吧。"

他们看见小鸟在表演杂技，狗狗骑着小马，还有一只打扮得像猫王埃尔维斯的黑猩猩，正对着麦克风"唱歌"呢。

看到驯虎师把手伸进老虎嘴巴里时，孩子们个个都被吓得倒吸了一口气。

"我猜这头老虎不饿。"乔希笑着说。

在小丑表演区，一个小丑打扮成一只长颈鹿，正踩着高跷跳舞。他和着音乐的节拍，让黄色吊裤带发出有节奏的噼啪声。

"我得赶紧回家啦。"过了一会儿，露丝说，"我妈妈要出去买东西，她让我在家里看着纳特。"

孩子们离开马戏团，穿过镇上的玫瑰园来到林荫街。

丁丁打了个响指："我突然想起来——我妈妈说我可以在我家后院搭帐篷。你们的爸爸妈妈允许你们在外面睡觉吗？"

"我没问题。"乔希说。

"纳特从来没有在帐篷里睡过,所以我会带他一起来。"露丝说。"还有泰格。"她甜甜地补充道。

"就你那个小弟弟!"乔希尖叫起来,"你可真行,这下我们都快有自己的马戏团了——一只

18

四岁的'猴子'和一只吃人的'老虎[1]'!"

露丝哈哈大笑起来:"别担心。我们会把自己的帐篷带过来的。"

---

1. 老虎:英文为 tiger,与露丝的猫咪"泰格"的英文名 Tiger 读音、拼写相同。此处乔希故意将泰格的名字理解为老虎。——译者

19

A to Z 神秘案件

丁丁和乔希把露丝送到她家门口，然后继续朝丁丁家走去。进了屋子，他们给戴维斯太太打了个电话。

"她说莫扎特还没回家呢。"丁丁挂断电话对乔希说。

他们两个正搭着帐篷，这时露丝来了，后面跟着他的小弟弟纳特。纳特拖着他那只破旧不堪的恐龙玩偶。

"嘿，你那只吃人的猫咪呢？"乔希问道。

露丝把帐篷放到地上。她的表情看起来就像刚刚咽下了什么难吃的东西。

"怎么了，露丝？"丁丁问道。

"泰格不见了。"露丝低声说，"我妈妈说它一整天都不在家。"

第二章

第二天一大早,露丝把头探进丁丁的帐篷喊道:"起床啦,两位!"

丁丁从一夜酣睡中醒了过来。"泰格回家了吗?"他一边问,一边睡眼惺忪地看着露丝。

"没呢,它还没回来。我打算去警察局,想要你们跟我一起去。"

乔希在睡袋里翻了个身:"去报失吗?说丢了一只猫咪?"

21

"不，我要报失的不只是一只猫咪，还有一只金丝雀。"露丝说完，把头从帐篷里退了出去。

丁丁和乔希你看看我，我看看你，紧接着爬出了帐篷。露丝正在草坪上来回踱步。

"两位，事情太奇怪了吧。"她说，"一天之内，一条街上有两只动物不见了！"露丝停下脚步看着他们，"我觉得莫扎特和泰格不是走丢了，而是被人偷走了。我现在把纳特送回家，然后你们跟我一起去找法伦警官报失。"

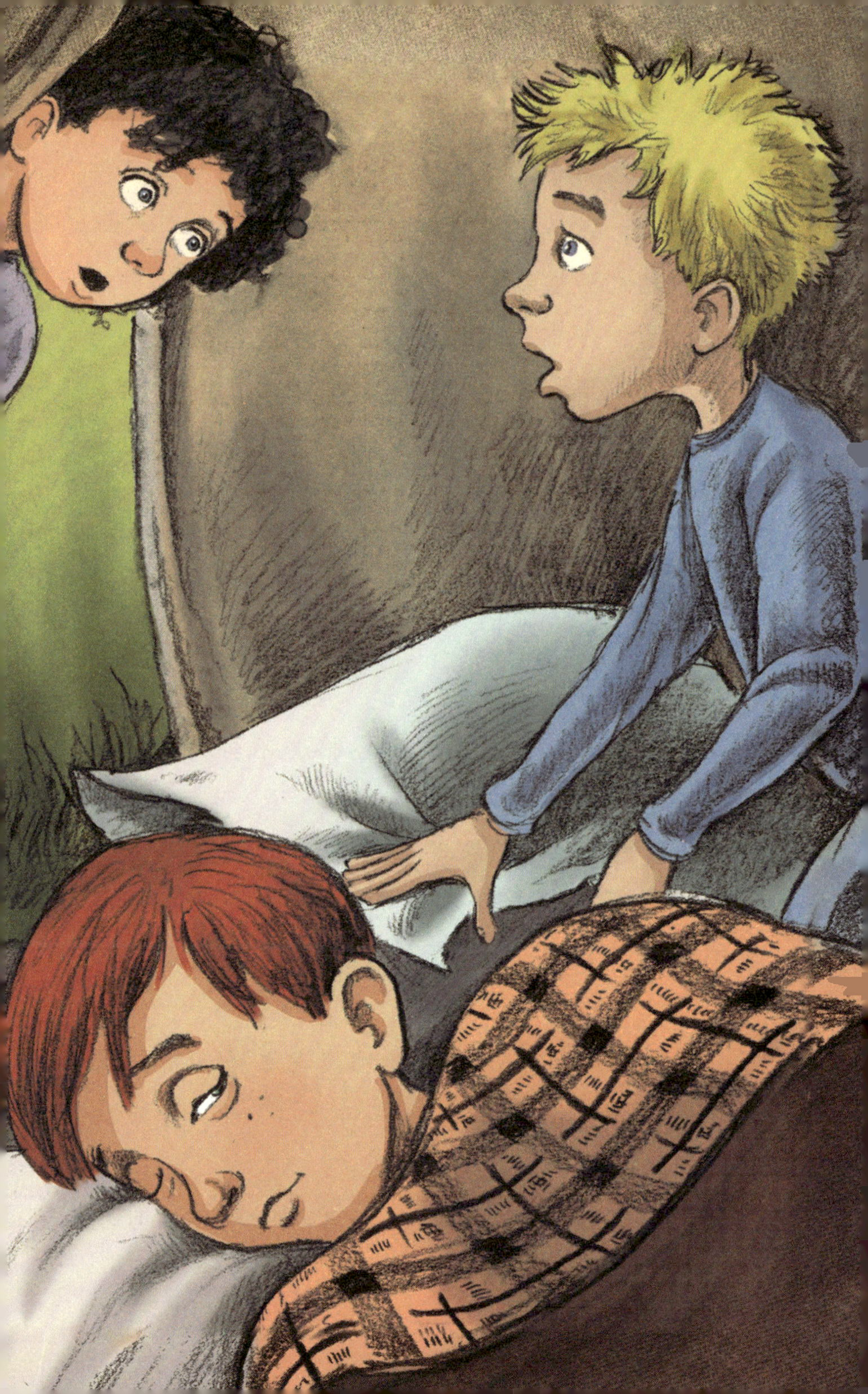

接着，露丝把纳特叫醒，拉着他的一只手，和他一起大踏步朝家里走去。

丁丁和乔希互相看着对方，耸了耸肩。随后他们走进丁丁家里，丁丁上楼到自己的房间换衣服，乔希则倒了两碗燕麦片。洛蕾塔，也就是丁丁的那只豚鼠，在笼子里发出吱吱的叫声，跟他打招呼。

丁丁回到楼下的时候，乔希正呼噜呼噜地喝着燕麦粥呢。

"我忍不住想，"乔希说，"假如是有人把这两只小动物一起偷走了，那泰格会不会把莫扎特吃掉呢？"

丁丁耸了耸肩。"我不知道。我甚至不能肯定泰格和莫扎特是被人偷走的。"他一边喝着燕麦粥，一边说，"可是露丝是我们的朋友，所以我们跟她一起去警察局吧。"

这时，露丝走了进来，她上身穿着一件红色衬衫，下身穿着一条蓝色短裤。"你们准备好出发了吗？"她问道。

丁丁睁大了眼睛，他从来没见过露丝同时穿

两种不同颜色的衣服。于是他给乔希递了个眼色，不过乔希正忙着看燕麦片的盒子的背面，根本没注意到这点。

"是的，我们准备好了。"丁丁一边说，一边把碗碟和玻璃杯放进水槽。

他们来到法伦警官的办公室，看见法伦警官正坐在办公桌前对着电脑打字，他喝着茶，嘴里还嚼着口香糖。

"嘿，大家好。"他一边打招呼，一边朝孩子们笑了笑，"这个周末打算去看马戏团表演吗？给你们一些免费入场票怎么样？"

"不用了，谢谢您，我们昨天已经去过了。"丁丁回答道。

法伦警官递给乔希三张票："再去一次嘛，绿地警察局请你们去！"

"法伦警官，我遇到了一个麻烦。"露丝开口说。

法伦警官用手指了指几张椅子："坐下来吧。我会好好地听你说。"

"是关于我的猫咪泰格的事情。它已经失踪

A to Z 神秘案件

整整一天一夜了。"露丝说,"它从来没有离开家这么长时间过!戴维斯太太的金丝雀也不见了!"

露丝的表情如此严肃,说话的腔调也是一本正经,这对丁丁来说还是头一次。

法伦警官在一张纸上记录着什么。

"我觉得绿地镇有人在偷宠物。"露丝继续说,"两只宠物在同一天消失,这太奇怪了!"

"是四只宠物,"法伦警官一边说,一边打开他的抽屉,抽出一张纸来,"已经有四只宠物失踪了。"

"四只?"丁丁和乔希异口同声地反问道。

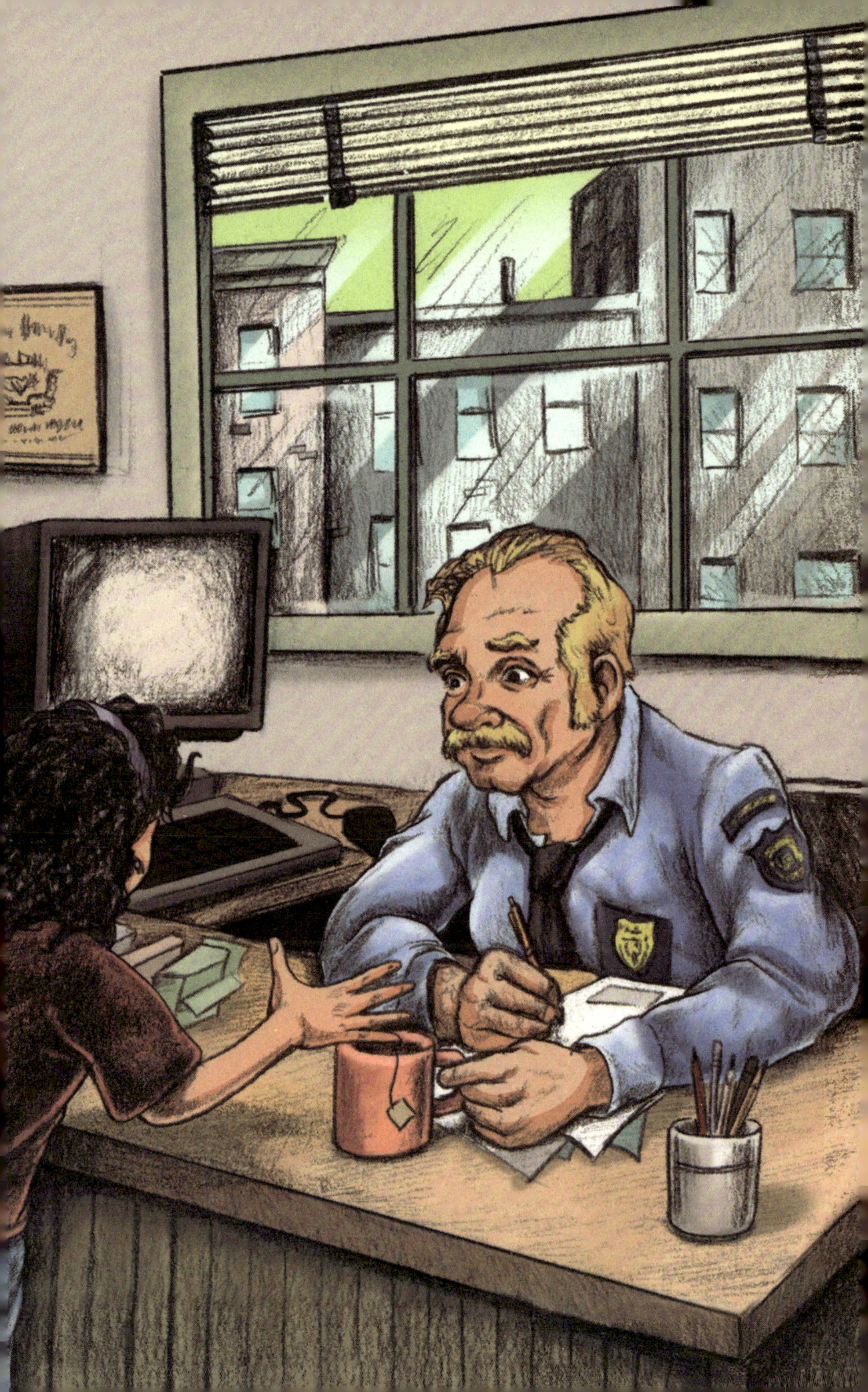

法伦警官点了点头:"昨天晚上,帕杜医生打来电话。他家孩子养的兔子从笼子里消失了。过了一会儿,格温太太打来电话,好像是说她养在屋后门廊上的鹦鹉也不见了。"

"全都是昨天丢的吗?"丁丁问道。

法伦警官点了点头。

"我猜得没错!"露丝说着就蹦了起来,"附近有一个偷宠物的贼!"

"同一天丢了四只宠物的确很奇怪。"法伦警官说,"实际上,我已经请基恩警官去调查这件事了。"

他看着露丝:"有没有可能你的猫咪只是外出度了个小假呢,露丝?我之前养过一只猫咪,它可喜欢出去流浪了。"

"好吧,泰格不是那样的猫咪。"露丝回答道,语气很坚定。

法伦警官点了点头。他告诉孩子们,一旦他有任何发现,会立刻通知他们。

孩子们离开警察局,朝着主街走去。

"听起来你可能猜对了,露丝。"丁丁说。

"或许我们应该去拜访一下宠物店的翁太太,以防万一。"乔希提议,"人们一直把流浪动物送到她那儿去。说不定有人发现了泰格,把它送到宠物店去了。"

露丝对乔希报以灿烂的笑容:"真是个好主意,乔希!"

他们经过霍华德理发店。霍华德正在门前清扫人行道。

"您看见我家那只橘色的大猫咪了吗?"露丝问他。

霍华德摇了摇头:"抱歉,露丝。"

毛脚宠物店的翁太太给了露丝同样的回答。"没有人把泰格送到店里来。"她说,"不过我会帮忙留意的。"

"戴维斯太太的金丝雀也丢了。"丁丁告诉翁太太。

"还有帕杜医生家的兔子和格温太太家的鹦鹉!"乔希补充道。

"丢了四只宠物吗?这确实太奇怪了!"翁太太扫视了一下自己的宠物店,"我想我应该把自己的小动物清点一下了。"

"我可以用一下您的电话吗,翁太太?"露丝问道,"我想给我妈妈打个电话,看看泰格回家了没有。"

"别客气,打吧。"翁太太说。

露丝拨了电话号码,轻声地跟她妈妈通了话,随后挂断了电话。

"泰格还没回家。"她说,"谁会想要偷走一只金丝雀、一只猫咪、一只鹦鹉和一只兔子呢?"

"我不知道。"丁丁说,"不过我们一定会把这件事弄个水落石出的!"

第三章

　　孩子们离开宠物店，朝主街走去。他们走得很慢，心里都在想着同一件事：接下来该怎么办。

　　"我以前看过科学家们把动物偷去做实验的报道。"乔希说。

　　"那太可怕了！"丁丁说。

　　"我可不想让泰格被用来做实验！"露丝说，"我们一定要找到这些动物。格温家和帕杜家在哪儿呢？"

　　"格温家离我们家不远，就在蓟花街。"丁

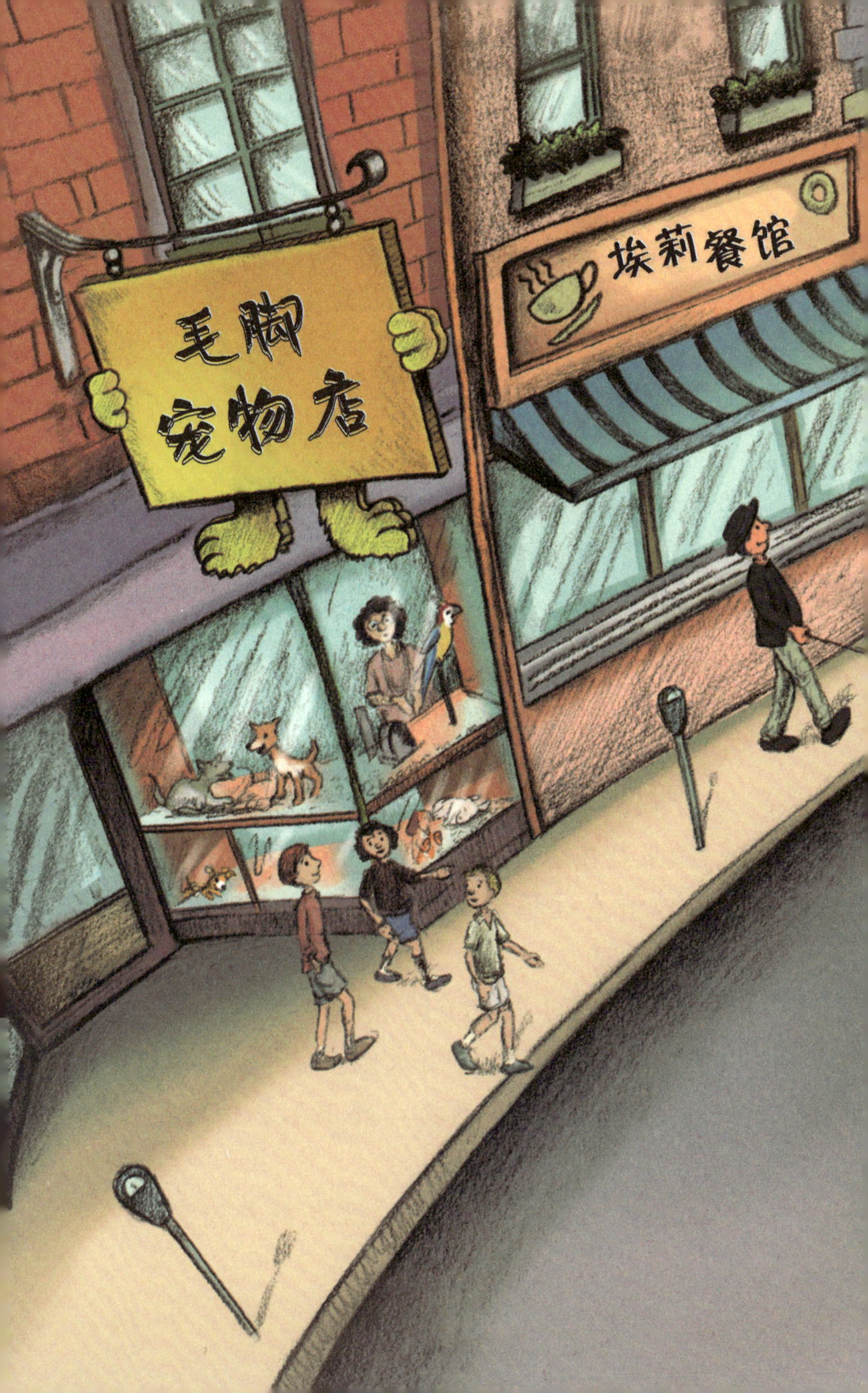
毛脚
宠物店
埃莉餐馆

丁说。

"我们过去跟他们聊聊吧。"露丝说,"说不定偷宠物的贼留下了一些蛛丝马迹。"

孩子们穿过了高中的操场,经过了马戏团的拖车。几个工作人员正坐在野餐桌前喝着咖啡,孩子们路过的时候,他们挥了挥手。

孩子们到达蓟花街的时候,露丝问道:"哪栋房子是格温家的?"

"那栋灰色的大房子。"乔希说。那栋房子门前的邮筒上写着"格温"两个黑色大字。

露丝走上台阶,按响门铃。格温太太打开了大门。

"嘿,孩子们!你们的夏天过得怎么样啊?"她问大家。

"不是特别开心。"露丝说,"昨天有人偷走了我的猫咪。"

"哦,露丝,真替你难过!昨天我的鹦鹉也不见了!"

"戴维斯太太的金丝雀也丢了。"乔希补充道。

"我们刚从警察局过来。"丁丁插话道,"法伦警官把您家丢了鹦鹉的事情跟我们说了。他还说帕杜医生家的兔子也丢了。"

格温太太张大了嘴巴:"我的天哪!你们的意思是,昨天有四只宠物不见了?"

"我们猜是这样的。"露丝说,"您最后一次看到您的鹦鹉是在哪里?"

"在我家屋后的门廊上,它当时在鸟笼里。"格温太太说。

"我们可以去看一看那个鸟笼吗?"丁丁问道。

格温太太领着孩子们穿过厨房,来到封闭式的门廊。只见门廊的一角立着一个鸟笼。

"阿奇喜欢待在这儿,"格温太太说,"它可以看到树上的其他鸟儿。可是昨天我来这里吃午餐的时候却发现它不见了。"

丁丁检查了通往后院的纱门。"当时这扇门上锁了吗?"他问。

"我真不记得了。这扇门我们经常不上锁。"格温太太说。

"那阿奇自己能把鸟笼的门打开吗?"乔希问道。

格温太太摇了摇头:"我们习惯在鸟笼的门上夹一个衣夹,确保它无法把门打开。"

"这么说,一定是有人把它偷走了。"露丝说。

"噢,天哪,我真不愿意相信绿地镇会出现犯罪分子。"格温太太一边说,一边叹着气,"你们几个要喝点什么吗?天气太热了。"

"不用了,谢谢。"露丝说,"请问我们可以借您家的电话簿查一下帕杜医生家的地址吗?"

A to Z 神秘案件

"他们家在野鸡巷3号。"格温太太说,"我经常送迈克去那里跟安迪·帕杜打网球。"

孩子们谢过格温太太,急匆匆朝主街走去。

"事情变得越来越奇怪了。"丁丁说,"光天化日之下,金丝雀和鹦鹉被人从鸟笼里抓出来,还是在主人在家的时候!"

"对了,泰格被人偷走时,它很可能正在我家后院玩。"露丝说。

他们朝角落书店的帕斯基先生挥挥手,前往鸟舍路。野鸡巷3号是一栋绿色的大房子,房子四面环绕着高高的树木。一个孩子坐在屋前的门廊里,手里拿着一个网球拍。

"嘿,"露丝一边打招呼,一边朝门廊走去,"请问帕杜医生在家吗?我们想要跟他聊聊他家兔子的事情。"

"我是安迪·帕杜。"孩子回答道,"维奥莱特是我养的兔子呢。怎么啦?你们找到它了吗?"

"没有,而且我的猫咪也丢了。"露丝说,"镇上还有两只宠物也丢了。"

丁丁朝帕杜家的前院看了看。"你家的兔子

是什么时候不见了的?"他问安迪。

"昨天午餐过后。"安迪说,"我妹妹尖叫着跑进屋子,于是我来到外面的兔笼边,只见兔笼的门大开着,维奥莱特不见了。"

"你能带我们去看看那个兔笼吗?"露丝问他。

安迪领着他们来到后院,一个空空的兔笼立在一棵树下。

"兔笼当时上锁了吗?"乔希问道。

"上锁了,每天晚上我都会亲自把它锁上。"安迪不满地瞪了他们一眼,"到底发生什么事了?难道出现了一个偷窃动物的团伙吗?"

"这正是我们想要弄清楚的事情。"丁丁说。

"好吧,你们找到什么线索告诉我一声。"安迪说,"天哪,我真想亲手把那个家伙抓起来。我的小妹妹哭了整整一个晚上呢。"

孩子们走回林荫街。

"我们进去跟戴维斯太太说一声吧。"孩子们经过戴维斯太太家时,丁丁建议,"我们应该把还有其他宠物丢失的情况告诉她一声。"

戴维斯太太打开家门的那一刻,脸上洋溢着

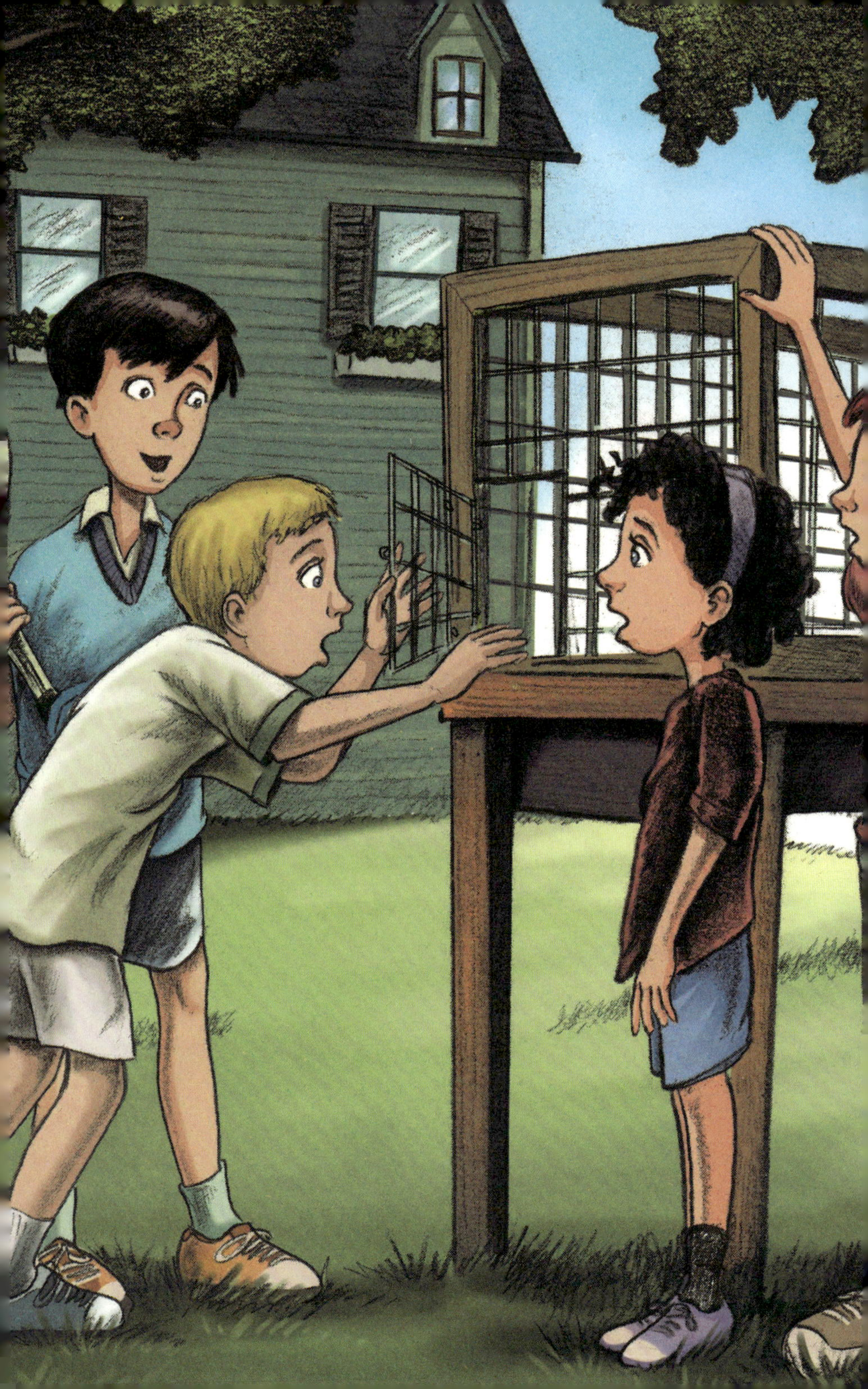

灿烂的笑容。

"哎哟,见到你们三个真是太高兴了!"她激动地大声说道,"你们无论如何也想不到!刚才有个男人打电话过来,说他发现莫扎特了!他会在六点半把我的金丝雀送回来。这是不是太令人开心了?"

"那可太好了。"丁丁看了一眼乔希和露丝,露出非常惊讶的表情。

"我希望你们三个在这儿待一会儿,因为你们心地善良,帮我寻找了莫扎特。"戴维斯太太接着说,"回头我们吃些草莓奶油酥饼庆祝吧!"

"太棒了!"乔希说。

"我们六点半再来拜访您吧。"丁丁一边说,一边挥了挥手。

三个孩子开始朝家里走去。

乔希笑着说:"我觉得莫扎特根本不是被人偷走的。"

"我也觉得不是。"丁丁一边附和,一边看了看露丝一眼。此刻,她没有笑。

"可是,有一件事我弄不明白。"最后她开口说,"那个人怎么知道该给谁打电话呢?他怎么知道莫扎特是谁家的呢?"

丁丁耸了耸肩:"说不定他是在戴维斯太太家附近发现莫扎特的,然后问了她家的哪个邻居。"

"或者,"露丝说,"打电话的人就是偷走莫扎特的那个人。"

"但是这样说不通啊。"丁丁说,"有人周四偷走了一只金丝雀,第二天又要还回去,他为什么要这样做?"

"为了得到奖赏。"露丝皱着眉头说,"这个家伙偷了别人家的宠物,再还回去,索要赏金。"

丁丁和乔希瞪大了眼睛看着露丝。

之后的路上,孩子们谁都没有再开口说话,默默地回家去了。

第四章

丁丁和露丝坐在丁丁家屋前的门廊里。他们刚刚吃完晚餐,正一起等着乔希。

露丝叹了一口气。

"泰格还没有回家吗?"丁丁问道。

她摇了摇头。

"猫咪有时候确实爱故意耍花招,使人迷惑。"丁丁说,他想让露丝心里好受些,"说不定它只是去什么地方见自己的猫咪小伙伴了呢。"

露丝耷拉着眼皮:"它可从来没有这样离开

过家。"

突然，丁丁注意到露丝忘记了系束发带。她的鬈发垂下来，遮住了眼睛。

正在这时，乔希从林荫街跑了过来，手里拿着一块画板。他慢跑着穿过丁丁家的草坪。

"泰格还没有回来吗？"他问道。

"没有呢。"露丝说着，站起身来，"走吧，我们去瞧瞧是谁把莫扎特送回去的。"

几分钟过后，他们按响了戴维斯太太家的门铃。露丝眼中露出坚定的光芒："如果那个家伙手上有被猫咪抓伤的痕迹，我就给法伦警官打电话。"

戴维斯太太打开门，可以看出，她特意打扮了一番。她项链上的绿色宝石在傍晚的阳光下闪闪发光。

"希望你们胃口大开。"她说，"为了让我们好好地庆祝莫扎特回家，我做了好多水果奶油酥饼呢。"

乔希笑着说："我说不定能吃下一小份。"

戴维斯太太哈哈大笑起来："哦，得了吧，约书亚·平托[1]。我已经见识过你是怎么吃掉我一炉饼干的了。"

孩子们来到客厅,莫扎特的空鸟笼就放在钢琴上。

"还能听到莫扎特唱歌真是太好了。"戴维斯太太说。

这时,门铃响了。"他来了!"戴维斯太太急匆匆朝门口走去。

一个瘦瘦的年轻人笑眯眯地站在屋前门廊上。只见他穿戴整洁,上身是一件白色衬衫,下身是一条黑色长裤,搭配着一副蓝色的吊裤带。

这个人手里提着一个小箱子,箱子的侧面被戳了几个小洞。"我是弗雷德·利特尔。"他说,"这是您的金丝雀。"

他把箱子递给戴维斯太太的时候,丁丁看了看这个人的两只手——一个被猫抓伤的痕迹也没有。随即丁丁瞥了露丝一眼。

"谢谢你,利特尔先生。"戴维斯太太说,"进

---

1. 乔希的全名。——编者

屋去坐坐吧。"

戴维斯太太向丁丁、乔希和露丝介绍了他。随后她打开箱子,把自己的金丝雀捧了出来。

"哎呀,莫扎特,你的假期过得怎么样啊?"她飞快地吻了一下金丝雀,然后把它放进鸟

笼里。

大家都停下来,看着莫扎特在鸟笼里跳来跳去,然后静下来整理自己的羽毛。

"利特尔先生,我简直无法形容我有多么感激您。"戴维斯太太说,"不过,您是如何知道该把它送回这儿的呢?"

露丝踢了一下丁丁的脚踝。

弗雷德·利特尔先生微微一笑。"我不得不

先做了一些侦察工作。"他说,"今天我给宠物店打了电话,询问镇上谁家养了金丝雀。一位好心的女士把您的姓名告诉了我,所以我在电话簿里找到了您的电话。"

"那一定是翁太太了。"丁丁说,"我们今天也去找她了解了一下情况,还告诉她露丝丢失了猫咪。您是什么时候给她打的电话?"

这人注视着丁丁。"我记不太清了,"他说,"在我发现金丝雀之后吧。"

戴维斯太太禁不住拍手称赞:"您费了这么大的周折,想得这么周到!您愿意接受赏金吗?"

露丝瞥了丁丁一眼,脸上露出得意的笑容。

这个人对戴维斯太太笑了笑。"您真是太好了,"他说,"不过不用谢我。对我来说,看到您的小鸟回家就是一种奖赏了。"

丁丁飞快地偷偷看了露丝一眼。她看上去一副迷惑不解的样子,丁丁知道她为什么会这样。

"如果他不接受赏金,那么莫扎特就不是他偷走的。如果莫扎特不是被人故意偷走的,泰格说不定也不是被人偷走的。"丁丁心里这样想。

"那您至少坐下来喝杯茶,吃点饼干吧。"戴维斯太太说。

"这样也好。"他说,"请问我可以用一下您家的洗手间吗?"

"沿着门厅往前走,在右手边。"戴维斯太太说,"孩子们,能去厨房帮帮我吗?"

戴维斯太太烧水、摆放银质茶具的时候,孩子们负责把饼干放到托盘里。

"他没有接受赏金。"露丝皱着眉头,轻声说,"我居然猜错了,真是不敢相信!"

"真想不到会是这样,露丝。"丁丁说,"但这家伙有些可疑。翁太太为什么没有告诉我们,他给她打过电话?"

"我们是上午去见的翁太太。"乔希提醒大家,"弗雷德·利特尔一定是之后才给她打电话的。"

"是的,我想应该是这样。"丁丁说。

"不过我还是有种怪怪的感觉,我之前好像在哪个地方见过弗雷德·利特尔。"乔希说。

"在这附近吗?"露丝问道。

乔希耸了耸肩:"我不敢确定。我也记不起来了。"

"你们三个在说什么悄悄话呢?"戴维斯太太喊道,"一会儿我就需要帮手啦。"

大家全都围着一张牌桌坐下来之后,戴维斯太太倒了五杯茶:"您只是路过这里吧,利特尔先生?我之前在镇上没见过您。"

"我是来这里找工作的。"弗雷德·利特尔说。

"这么说,您有可能在绿地镇定居?那真是太好了!"

弗雷德·利特尔微微笑了笑。"这是个不错的镇子。"他一边说,一边环顾客厅,"您家布置得很温馨,戴维斯太太。"

"啊,谢谢夸奖。我丈夫在世的时候,我们常常去旅行。"戴维斯太太说,"每到一个国家,我们都会带回来一些特别的东西。"

几分钟过后,弗雷德·利特尔离开了,孩子们帮着戴维斯太太把桌子收拾干净。"还能再吃一些水果奶油酥饼吗?"她笑着问乔希。

"当然可以啦!"乔希回答着,拿起了他的画板。

乔希开始画弗雷德·利特尔的面部画像:"真希望我能记起来之前在哪里见过这个家伙。"

第五章

那天晚上突然下起了雷阵雨,孩子们只得从帐篷里钻出来,跑回屋子里。

第二天,雨继续下着,因此他们决定在丁丁家玩大富翁游戏棋。

"露丝,轮到你了。"乔希说。

"我知道。"她说着,眼睛盯着窗外,"我没法集中注意力。这个时候泰格正在外面淋着雨呢。"

听到她这样说,丁丁和乔希两个人面面相觑。

"如果弗雷德·利特尔没偷宠物,那么会是

谁偷走了宠物呢?"露丝问道。她走过来,一屁股坐在大富翁游戏棋的棋盘上。

丁丁想了想。"如果能弄明白那人为什么要偷走宠物,"他说,"说不定我们就能搞清楚是谁干的呢。"

露丝拿起她的一沓大富翁游戏币。"我还是觉得偷宠物的人是为了钱。"她说,"绑架这种事,通常是为了赎金,没错吧?"

两个男孩点了点头。

"但是没有人在丢了宠物之后收到勒索信。"乔希说。

"至少现在还没有。"露丝把她的游戏币扔在桌子上,"我要回家了。我妈妈在报纸上登了一则寻猫启事,万一有人打电话过来告知泰格的情况,我想第一时间知道。"

两个男孩看着她穿上外套,一头扎进了雨中。

"我从来没见过她这样闷闷不乐。"门被关上后,乔希说,"她甚至都不想跟我争辩了!"

"没错。还有,她今天也没有穿同一种颜色的衣服,你注意到了吗?"丁丁指出这一点,"真希望泰格赶快回家。"

那天晚上雨停了,所以丁丁和乔希又睡在了屋子外面的帐篷里。

第二天早上,露丝把他们叫醒。只见她上身穿着一件旧T恤衫,下身穿着裤腿被剪短了的牛仔裤,脚上穿着运动鞋,鞋带松开了,拖在地上,沾的都是泥巴。

"看看这个吧,两位。"她一边说,一边把一份《周末晨报》递到丁丁面前。

其中一段文字被红色蜡笔圈了起来。丁丁和乔希跌跌撞撞地钻出帐篷,坐在野餐桌边。

这段文字出自"本地犯罪案件"栏目。丁丁匆匆扫了一遍,随即大声朗读出来:

"查尔斯·法伦警官说,昨天晚上绿地镇有两户人家遭遇入室盗窃。迈克尔·帕杜夫妇和哈维·格温夫妇的家有陌生人潜入,好几件贵重物品被盗。警方正在调查中。"

丁丁抬起头:"哇!一开始,他们丢了宠物,接下来,有人潜入他们家中。我觉得这真是太糟糕了!"

"还有，我觉得这几件事是相互关联的。"露丝说，"难道你们没看出来吗？全都是为了钱！有人偷走了这两户人家的宠物，接着潜入这两户人家进行了盗窃。"

"可是，那人为什么要先偷宠物，再入室盗窃呢？"丁丁不解地问。

"不只是这一点让人无法理解。"乔希补充道，"你家和戴维斯太太家又是什么情况？你们两家的宠物不见了，可是你们两家并没有遭遇入室盗窃。"

"他说的没错，露丝。"丁丁说，"遭遇入室盗窃的为什么只有两户人家，而不是丢失宠物的四户人家？"

露丝对着丁丁和乔希皱起了眉头。"我不知道。"她说。

"我们应该想办法将这件事弄个水落石出。现在我们再去拜访一次帕杜家和格温家吧。说不定窃贼留下了一些蛛丝马迹！"

他们匆匆来到蓟花街，按响了门铃。格温先生穿着浴袍过来开了门。

"噢，嘿，孩子们！格温太太跟我说你们周五来过了。你们猜怎么着？昨天下午有人发现了我们家的鹦鹉，把它送回来了！"

露丝盯着格温先生："昨天有人把阿奇送回来了吗？"

格温先生点了点头："为了庆祝这件事，我带家人出去吃了晚餐，看了电影。不过，我们回到家的时候，就发现家里被盗了。这帮卑鄙之徒把我收藏的硬币偷走了。"

"听到您这么说，我真难过。"丁丁说。

"您能告诉我是谁把鹦鹉还回来的吗？"

"是一位好心的年轻女士。"格温先生告诉孩子们，"她说她发现阿奇在她的鸟食盆下面吃果核呢。"

"您有邀请她进屋吗？"露丝问道。

还没等格温先生回答，丁丁便脱口而出："她之前见过您收藏的硬币吗？"

格温先生张大了嘴巴。"你的意思是……噢，天哪，你可能真的猜对了！"他说，"我收藏的硬币就放在客厅，在我们当时坐着聊天的地方。你

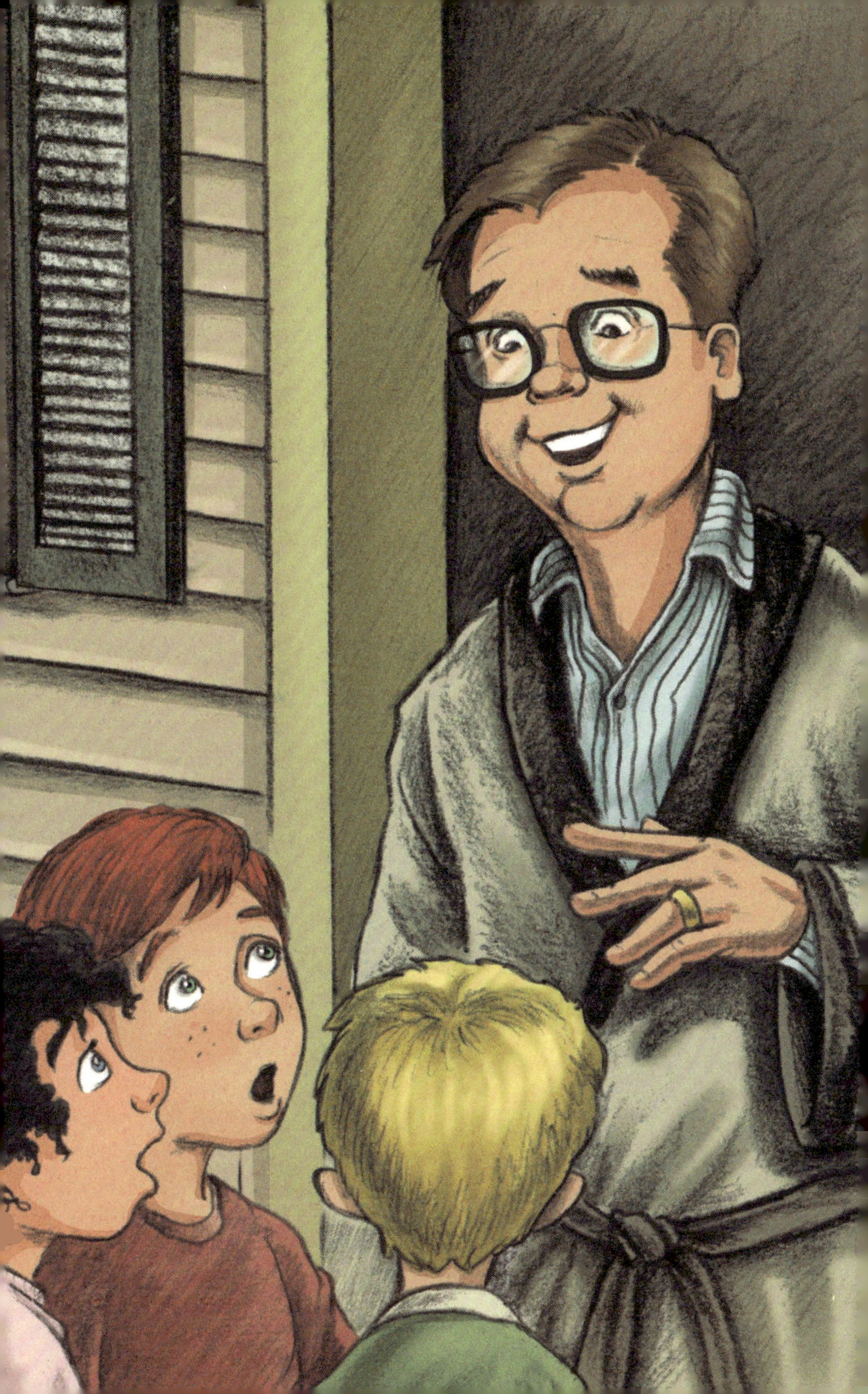

觉得是她把藏品偷走的吗?"

丁丁、乔希和露丝你看看我,我看看你。露丝脸上露出一副"我早就跟你们说过"的表情。

"看起来确实是这样的,格温先生。"丁丁说。

孩子们谢过格温先生,一路跑步前进,来到帕杜家。露丝累得上气不接下气,按响了门铃。

帕杜太太前来开了门。"嘿,孩子们,有什么事吗?"她说。

露丝问道:"请问昨天您家被盗之前,有没有什么人把您家的兔子送回来?"

"哎呀,你是怎么知道的?"帕杜太太说道,"一对好心的年轻夫妇打来电话,说他们在自己家的花园里发现了维奥莱特。昨天下午他们把它送回来了。"

丁丁把格温先生家的鹦鹉在他们家遭遇入室盗窃前也被送回来的情况给帕杜太太讲了一遍。

帕杜太太瞪大了眼睛:"跟我家的情况一模一样!那对年轻夫妇进了屋,跟我们一起喝了冷饮。帕杜医生要给他们赏金来着,不过被他们拒绝了。"

"他们偷走了什么东西？"乔希问道。

"我的几件贵重首饰，"帕杜太太说，"其中有我祖母留给我的。"

露丝思索了一会儿说："他们有要求过使用您家的洗手间吗？"

"有，是那位女士问的。"帕杜太太回答道，"她很可能就在那时窥探了我的卧室。我怎么那么傻啊！"

孩子们告别了帕杜太太，奔主街而去。

"我早就知道！"露丝说，"偷宠物的贼和入室盗窃的贼是同一伙人！"

"好家伙，多么卑鄙的骗局啊。"乔希说，"他们偷走了别人家的宠物，趁着送还宠物的机会了解别人家的情况，再返回去偷走他们喜欢的东西。"

"已经发生两起案件了。"丁丁说着摇了摇头。

"我觉得会有第三起案件。"露丝说，"还有戴维斯太太家呢。"

"她家怎么了？"乔希问道，"她家还没……

噢,我的天哪!"

"没错。"露丝说,"我敢打赌,窃贼的下一个目标就是戴维斯太太家!"

第六章

"或者,下一个目标是你家。"丁丁提醒露丝说。

露丝摇了摇头:"他们还没把泰格送回来,所以他们还没有进过我家。快点,我们必须把这些情况告诉法伦警官!"

孩子们沿着主街一路跑到了警察局。

"周日上午他上班吗?"他们匆匆走上台阶时,乔希问道。

"等会儿我们就知道了。"丁丁说。

孩子们差点跟正要出门的法伦警官撞个满怀。

"你们几个是来找我的吗？"他问道，"我正要去埃莉餐馆呢。"

"法伦警官，我们查出了入室盗窃案的真相！"露丝大声说。

法伦警官看着她："是吗？那我们还是回屋里谈吧。"

法伦警官坐到办公桌前，拿起一支铅笔。"说吧，我听着呢。"他说。

露丝将他们的推测告诉了他，那些偷宠物的人如何把宠物还给主人，然后潜入他们的家进行盗窃。

法伦警官笑了笑。"你们的推测是对的。"他说，"我也是这么想的。"

"戴维斯太太的金丝雀也被送回去了，您知道吗？"露丝问完，看了一眼丁丁和乔希，"我们觉得她家是盗贼的下一个目标。"

法伦警官的眉毛向上扬了扬。"好吧，这的确是个新消息。我还不知道金丝雀的事。它是什么时候被送回去的？"他一边问，一边在便笺簿上写着什么。

"周五,"乔希说,"有个家伙打电话说他发现了莫扎特。他把莫扎特送回去的时候我们刚好在那儿。"

法伦警官瞪大了眼睛。"给我描述一下这个人,乔希。"他轻声说。

乔希描述着这个人的外貌特征,法伦警官继续在便笺簿上做着记录。

"在弗雷德·利特尔进入戴维斯太太家盗窃之前,您可以逮捕他吗?"露丝问道。

法伦警官敲了敲铅笔,眯起一只眼睛看着孩子们:"基恩警官和我一直在寻找是谁把格温家和帕杜家的宠物送回去的。我们想要询问他们有关偷窃宠物和入室盗窃的情况。现在我们也要开始寻找弗雷德·利特尔了。"

他撑着胳膊肘,身体向前倾:"不过我们没有证据证明这些人干了坏事。弗雷德·利特尔同样是这样。没错,他把金丝雀送了回去,并进入了利昂娜·戴维斯的家,这与另外两起入室盗窃案的情况相同,但够不上犯罪。"

"您不能逮捕他吗?"乔希问道。

法伦警官摇了摇头:"就算我知道到哪里能找到弗雷德·利特尔,我也没有证据证明他正在谋划犯罪活动。"

"可是,我们总得做点什么吧。"露丝说。

"你们已经做了很多了。"法伦警官说,"我之前不知道利昂娜·戴维斯的金丝雀已经被人送回去了,是你们给我提供了一条重要的线索。基恩警官和我非常感谢你们的帮助,孩子们。"

他把孩子们送到门口:"别担心,我们还有一些小妙招来对付这些坏蛋。"

"我还是觉得我们应该做点什么。"孩子们来到室外,露丝说。

"嗯……"乔希说,"马戏团明天就要离开了,法伦警官给我们的那些免费票还在……"

丁丁哈哈大笑起来,他和乔希一起说服了露丝,花几个小时去看马戏团表演。

他们观看了几场动物表演,买了爆米花。

露丝不想乘坐任何游乐设施,所以他们决定再次进去小丑帐篷观看表演。

舞台上,一座纸板做成的小型建筑"着火"

了，两个小丑扮成消防员，四处奔跑，你撞我来我撞你。

烟雾和假的火焰从一扇窗户里冒了出来。一个女小丑尖叫着："救命啊！救救我！"

这时候，观众席上的几个孩子开始大声喊道："救救她，先生！在那上面，救救她！"

扮演消防员的两个小丑被自己的水管缠住了，这让大家笑得更厉害了，喊叫声也更加响亮了。

突然，一个扮成超人的小丑踩着高跷出来了。只见他穿着一件蓝色衬衫，外面披着一件红色披风，亮黄色的吊裤带吊着一条蓝色紧身裤，紧身裤遮住了他的高跷。

超人哗啦一下甩起他的披风，噼啪一声弹起他的吊裤带，然后朝着着火的建筑大步走去，救了那位女士。观众中所有的孩子都欢呼着鼓起了掌。

丁丁注意到，露丝几乎没在看这些表演。于是他用手肘轻轻地推了推乔希，随即，他们离开了现场。

"我想要一些高跷。"乔希一边说，一边控制

A to Z 神秘案件

着双腿,笔直而僵硬地走了起来,还用手弹着想象中的、无形的吊裤带,"马戏团会招孩子吗?"

"会招啊,招了去喂老虎。"丁丁说着,想起了露丝那只名叫泰格的猫咪。他看了露丝一眼:"你想不想来我家把大富翁游戏棋玩完?"

金丝雀之谜

她摇了摇头:"你们两个难道不想解开这个谜团吗?"

"当然想,可是我们还能做什么呢?"丁丁说,"法伦警官说过,他会去找归还宠物的人。"

"嗯,我知道我们该怎么帮助他了。"露丝说,眼睛里闪烁着光芒。

"哎呀。"乔希咕哝。

"嗯,露丝,我觉得法伦警官不需要任何帮助了。"丁丁说。

露丝没有理会他的话。"你们两个今天晚上还要睡在帐篷里吗?"她问道。

丁丁点了点头:"我想是的。怎么啦?"

露丝咧着嘴笑了,显得神秘兮兮的:"如果你们答应跟我一起去一个地方,我保证给你们带饼干过来。"

"去哪儿?"丁丁问她,"为什么你脸上露出一副鬼鬼祟祟的表情?"

"穿上黑色的衣服吧。"露丝说,"我们要去监视戴维斯太太的家!"

第七章

"监视?"乔希惊讶地问道。

露丝点了点头。

"像警察电影里演的那样吗?"丁丁问道。

她又点了点头。

"你觉得戴维斯太太家今天晚上会被盗吗?"乔希问。

露丝第三次点了点头。"所以我打算到那里去看看是谁干的。"她咧着嘴笑了,"这样的证据对法伦警官来说足够充分了吧?"

"假设确实来了一个入室窃贼,"丁丁说,"我们该怎么做呢,把他绑起来吗?"

"肯定的啊!"乔希说,"我负责带绳子吧。"

露丝摇了摇头:"不需要绳子。我们只需要坐着观望就行了。如果有人来,我们当中的一个人跑去警察局,其余两个人继续蹲守。如果那个家伙离开,我们就跟踪他。"

丁丁仔细想了想:"跟踪他到哪里去?"

"他去哪里,我们就跟踪到哪里,丁丁。说不定他会带我们去他藏匿赃物的地方。"露丝说,"还有,那个地方说不定就是他藏泰格的地方。"

"嗯,我觉得这一招能管用,只要我们把那个家伙盯住了。"丁丁说。

露丝点了点头:"我们只需要耐心等待,仔细观察。"

"还有吃着饼干。"乔希补充道。

丁丁和乔希坐在黑洞洞的帐篷里等待着露丝。此时已经差不多十点钟了。

乔希穿着黑色T恤衫和迷彩裤,丁丁则穿着深灰色的运动衫和牛仔裤。

金丝雀之谜

"她到底在哪儿?"乔希问道。

丁丁从帐篷门帘向外面看去:"如果我爸爸妈妈看到我们大晚上的在绿地镇跑来跑去,会杀了我的。"

"我爸爸妈妈会关我十年禁闭。"乔希说,"我们为什么要听她的话?为什么要做这种事?"

突然,丁丁听到了什么声响。"你听到什么动静了吗?"他低声问道。

乔希朝外面瞥了一眼:"露丝?是你吗?"

"嘿!"露丝咯咯地笑了起来,"我就在这儿呢,乔希。"

丁丁把头伸到帐篷外面,不过他什么也没看到。"得了吧,露丝,别闹了。你躲在哪儿啊?"

"我才没有躲呢。"突然间,丁丁看见了她。露丝坐在离他大约四英尺[1]远的地方,就在他正对面。她身穿黑色夹克和黑色牛仔裤,用滑雪帽把头发遮住了。她甚至把脸都涂黑了。除了她的眼白,露丝几乎隐形了。

---

1. 英尺:英美制长度单位。1英尺=0.3048米。——编者

A to Z 神秘案件

"你脸上涂的是什么东西?"丁丁好奇地问她。

"液体鞋油。"她从双肩背包里拿出来一个瓶子,"给,涂一些到脸上吧。"

"必须得涂吗?"丁丁问道。

"没错!月光之下,万一入室窃贼看到你们那两张闪闪发光的大白脸怎么办?"

于是丁丁倒了一些鞋油在手上,然后在脸上涂抹开。"这东西好臭啊。"他咕哝着。

乔希也跟着这样做了。"我觉得自己像英雄兰博[1]。"他说。此时此刻,丁丁看见乔希洁白的牙齿在闪闪发光。

"我们出发吧。"露丝说着,悄悄离开了帐篷。

两个男孩跟在她后面,沿着林荫街往前走。他们悄悄溜进戴维斯太太家的后院,看见屋子里面一片漆黑。丁丁尽量不去想他们正在做的事情。

露丝把他们躲藏的地点选好了,是房子后面两丛茂密的灌木丛之间的一片昏暗地带。

1.电影《第一滴血》的男主角。——编者

当晚几乎是满月，不过月亮前有大团的云朵持续飘过。孩子们在草坪上扭来扭去，渐渐感到舒适、放松。

"你带饼干了吗?"乔希问露丝。

"带了，不过我们要等会儿再吃。"露丝说，"说不定我们要在这儿待上好几个小时呢。"

乔希深深地叹了一口气："说话不算话的大骗子……"

"她说的没错，乔希。"丁丁小声地说。

"对了，我觉得我们不要再说话了。万一入室窃贼来了，说不定他听到我们的说话声就转身离开了呢。"

五秒钟过去了。

"只吃一小块饼干而已，又不会把你带的东西全部吃光，露丝。"

"乔希，我们这是在监视，不是在埃莉餐馆用餐。"

"警察监视的时候也要吃东西啊。"

"乔希！嘘！"

丁丁张开手脚，四仰八叉地躺在草地上，注

视着房子后面，观察有没有移动的影子。不过，没有什么东西在动。

他打到了一只蚊子。

一只白猫悠闲地在院子里走过。

丁丁打起了哈欠。

每隔几分钟，他就要看一下手表。

最后他把眼睛闭上了。

等他重新睁开眼睛时，时间差不多到十一点钟了。乔希睡得正香，不过丁丁看到露丝的眼睛睁得大大的。

"你肚子饿了吗？"她小声地问丁丁。

他点了点头，摇了摇乔希的肩膀。

露丝打开双肩背包，拿出一袋饼干，三根香蕉，以及三盒苹果汁。

孩子们一声不吭地吃着东西，同时倾听着，监视着，以防入室窃贼出现。

"谢谢，露丝。"乔希小声说。随即他重新仰躺在草地上，闭上双眼。

丁丁打了个哈欠，想让自己舒服点。他多么希望自己带了睡袋啊。他的睡袋又软又……突然，他看到房子旁边的阴影里有什么东西在动。

他摇了摇乔希,把嘴巴凑到露丝的耳朵旁。"快看。"他小声说着,用手指着一个方向。

不过他看到的东西现在又不动了。

丁丁的眼睛盯着房子后面。他看到的只是树木和灌木丛的影子。

突然,其中的一个影子动了。

丁丁闻到了从乔希嘴巴里飘出来的饼干味。"窃贼来了!"乔希小声地说。丁丁能感觉到乔希兴奋得浑身都在发抖。

丁丁的心猛地往下一沉。一个身穿黑衣服、头戴棒球帽的人蹑手蹑脚地来到戴维斯太太的房子后面。他挎着一个健身包,两只手握着一根长杆。因为窃贼躲在昏暗处,丁丁看不见他的脸。

这时,窃贼把他的包和长杆放到地上,在房子后面检查了一下一楼的每扇窗户。发现窗户全都被锁住了之后,他绕到房子侧面,消失不见了。

"我们现在该怎么办?"乔希问道,"他是要离开吗?"

丁丁摇了摇头:"他的东西还在呢。"

金丝雀之谜

"你们有谁能认得出他吗?"露丝问道。

谁也认不出。突然,那个黑影又回来了。他背对着孩子们站在那里,抬头看着房子。

突然,窃贼转过身来,仿佛在直勾勾地看着丁丁。

让丁丁感到庆幸的是,他刚才把自己的脸抹黑了。突然,乔希一把抓住丁丁的一条胳膊:"果真是送还金丝雀的那个家伙!"

露丝倒吸了一口气。

弗雷德·利特尔正朝他们走来!

第八章

丁丁尝试退回到两丛灌木丛之间的昏暗地带。他感觉乔希和露丝也在这样做。

弗雷德·利特尔越走越近,丁丁的心怦怦直跳。突然,弗雷德·利特尔停下脚步,脱下夹克,把它挂在离丁丁的鼻子三英尺远的一根树枝上。接着,他朝着房子走过去。

乔希一把抓住丁丁:"快看,他身上吊着黄色吊裤带呢。"

丁丁想起了之前在什么地方看见过这种吊裤带。他朝乔希咧着嘴笑了:"是那个超人小丑!"

"还有那个长颈鹿小丑。"乔希小声地回应丁丁,"我就知道我之前见过他。"

孩子们看着弗雷德·利特尔打开他的健身包,拿出一卷绳子套在自己的脖子上。

随后,他拿起自己随身携带的那根长长的杆子。事实上,那并不是一根杆子。

弗雷德·利特尔随身携带的是一副长长的高跷。只见他小心翼翼地把高跷斜靠在房子上,然后迅速踩上脚踏板。现在,他大约有十英尺那么高了,只见他踩着高跷走到二楼的一个小窗户下面。

过了一会儿,丁丁看到弗雷德·利特尔悄悄地从窗户钻了进去。一开始他只是踩着高跷站在那儿,随即他就不见了,像一条蛇溜进了洞里。

他的高跷还靠在房子的一侧。

乔希凑到丁丁的耳边说:"我们是不是应该——"

"嘘,等一等。"露丝小声地说。

突然,一根绳子从窗户上垂落下来。绳子的一头垂在了地面上,落在两根高跷中间。

"他肯定是想要顺着绳子滑下来。"露丝说。

"我们把绳子和高跷拿走吧,"乔希小声地说,"这样他就被困在里面了!"

"可是戴维斯太太也在屋子里。"露丝说,"我们一定得让他出来,然后跟踪他。"

"现在,我们当中必须有一个人跑到警察局去。"丁丁说。

可问题是,谁也不愿意错过这个激动人心的时刻。

突然,有三件事情同时发生了:楼上的灯亮了,丁丁听见有人在大声尖叫,敞开的窗户里传出了响亮刺耳的警哨声。

丁丁跳了起来,不知道该怎么办。戴维斯太太在楼上,窃贼很可能跟她待在同一个房间里!

可是,尖叫声是谁发出来的呢?

丁丁看见窗户上出现了一个影子。过了一会儿,弗雷德·利特尔顺着他的逃生绳爬了下来。还没等双脚着地,他就掉下去了。

后院突然间变得五彩缤纷,同时爆发出一阵嘈杂声。

一辆巡逻警车呼啸着穿过戴维斯太太家的草

坪，红、黄、蓝三色的警灯闪烁着。后院看上去就像在举办一场烟花表演。

警笛声响起，盖过了尖锐的警哨声。

就在巡逻警车车门被打开的那一刻，嘈杂声停了下来。法伦警官和基恩警官跳下了警车。

"不许动！"法伦警官大喊道。

弗雷德·利特尔还蹲在先前跳下来的地方呢。丁丁看见他的嘴巴大张着，一副惊慌失措的样子。

几秒钟后，他被戴上了手铐。

就在基恩警官押着窃贼走向巡逻警车时，戴维斯太太家的后门突然开了。只见戴维斯太太穿着白色睡袍和松软的拖鞋快步走了出来。她穿过院子朝弗雷德·利特尔走去，拖鞋发出啪嗒啪嗒的响声。

她的脸由于涂了白色乳液而闪着亮光，她的头上戴着一顶蕾丝边帽子。此外，她手里握着一把长刀，将它高高地举过头顶。

"你胆子真够大的！"她冲着一脸惊恐的弗雷德·利特尔大声喊道，"竟敢闯进我的卧室！"

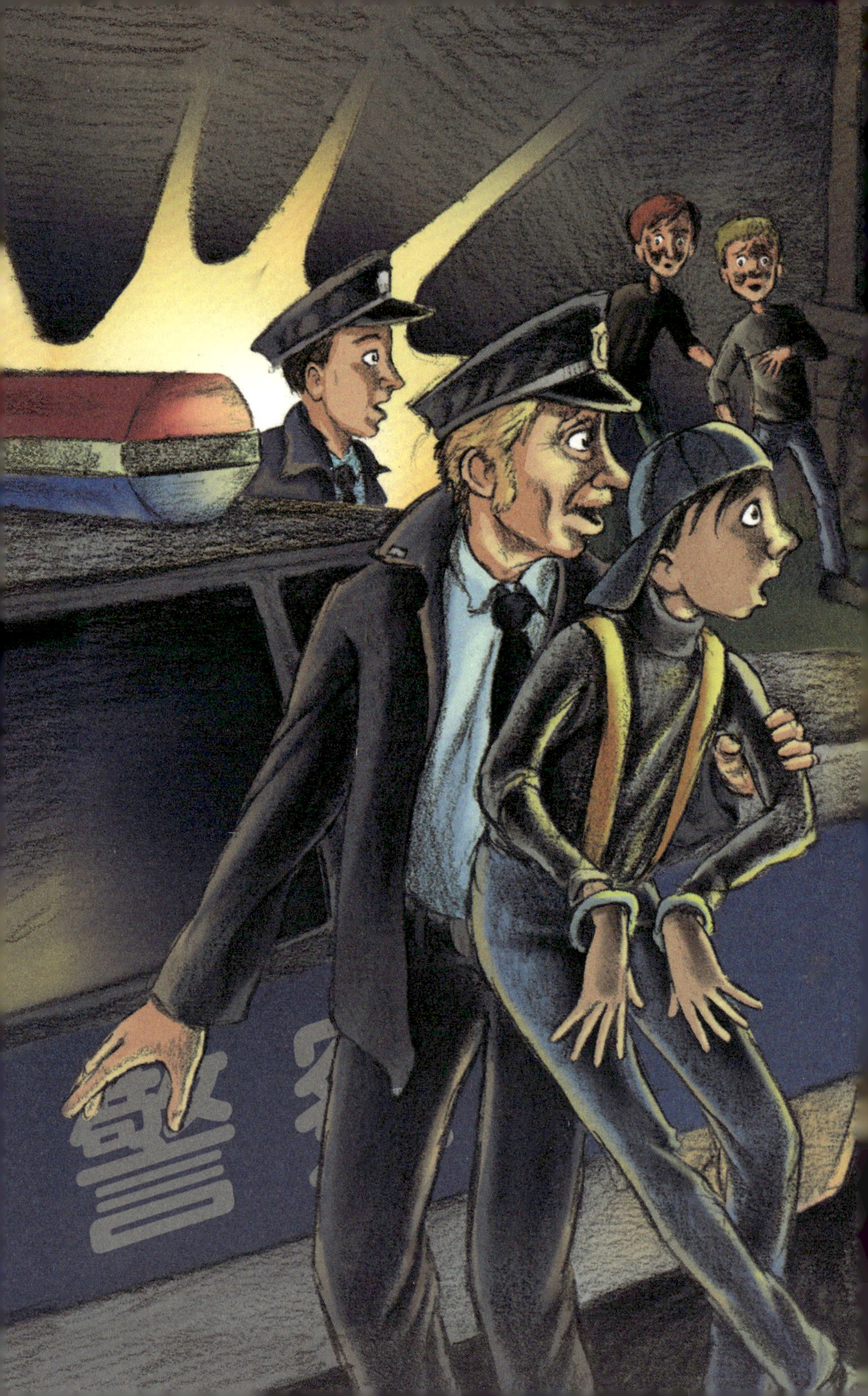
警

那把长刀在巡逻警车前灯的照耀下闪闪发亮。丁丁还以为戴维斯太太要用它来对付窃贼。

"我听说你在找我的珠宝?!"她喊道,"我之前还用茶水和饼干招待过你!"

"出来吧。"露丝突然大喊。

在场的每一个人,尤其是弗雷德·利特尔,看到三个"小忍者"从灌木丛中爬出来,都惊讶极了。

第九章

露丝踏着重重的步伐走到弗雷德·利特尔跟前,两只眼睛愤怒地瞪着他。"我的泰格在哪里?"她问道。

弗雷德·利特尔吓得往后退了几步:"什么老虎[1]?"

"就是我的宠物猫咪。是你把它给偷走了

---

[1] 老虎:英文为 tiger,与露丝的猫咪"泰格"的英文名 Tiger 读音、拼写相同(见第 19 页脚注)。此处弗雷德·利特尔把猫咪的名字理解成了老虎,故而吓得往后退。——译者

吧？它现在在哪儿？"

"我才没偷什么猫咪呢。"他咕哝着,"我对猫毛过敏。"

"你们在这儿干什么？"法伦警官皱着眉头问道。

"我们觉得今天晚上有人想要入室盗窃，"露丝一边说，一边指着窃贼，"我们想拿到证据，这样你们就可以把他抓起来。"

"这个人叫弗雷德·利特尔，"乔希说，"就是把金丝雀送回给戴维斯太太的那个家伙。他也是马戏团的一个小丑。"

"此外，他可能也是盗窃帕杜医生家和格温家的那个人。"丁丁补充道。

"看起来的确是这样。"法伦警官说。随即他吩咐基恩警官把弗雷德·利特尔锁在巡逻警车里，开车离开。

法伦警官表情严肃地看着丁丁。"有什么事我们明天再说吧。"他说，"你们几个最好赶紧回家睡觉去。"

"胡说！"戴维斯太太说，"这几个孩子再待一会儿也没事。我自己是一点也睡不着了!进屋里来吃点饼干,喝点可可饮料吧。大家都进来吧。"

法伦警官微笑着摇了摇头。大家跟着戴维斯太太进了厨房。丁丁注意到,莫扎特的鸟笼就放在操作台上。

戴维斯太太把水烧开,从橱柜里拿出几个马克杯。然后她打开了鸟笼的盖子。莫扎特叽叽喳喳地叫着,眨巴着它那双小小的黑眼睛。

"你真是给大家添了不少麻烦啊。"她对金丝雀说。

"事实上,利昂娜,您家的金丝雀帮助我们侦破了一起连环盗窃案呢。"法伦警官说,"我打探到了许多关于弗雷德·利特尔和他女朋友的事情。他们随马戏团巡回演出,并在他们到访的每个镇子实施盗窃,已经有一段时间了。他们的作案手段始终如此。首先,他们偷走人家的宠物;接着,他们把宠物还回去,目的是偷看人家家里的情况;然后,他们对这些人家实施盗窃。"

戴维斯太太摇了摇头:"你们真该看看我开灯的时候那个鬼鬼祟祟的窃贼脸上的表情。不过,他是怎么知道我楼上洗手间的窗户是打开的呢?"

"可能他在偷走您的金丝雀的时候就看见窗户是打开的了。"法伦警官说。

"或者是他把窗户打开的。"丁丁说,"之前他用您的洗手间时可能偷偷溜上楼了。"

"或许你说的对,丁丁。"法伦警官说,"他踩着高跷,可以够得到楼上的窗户,大多数人都不会给楼上的窗户上锁。在盗窃行当中,这类窃贼被称为'二楼窃贼'。"

"从今天晚上起,"戴维斯太太说,"那扇窗户要上锁了!"

"您怎么知道弗雷德·利特尔今天晚上会入室盗窃呢?"丁丁好奇地问。

"我们把巡逻警车停在了附近。"法伦警官继续说,"我们是这样想的,他们要么不偷窃,要偷窃就一定是在今天晚上,因为马戏团明天就要离开镇子了。"

突然,门口传来敲门声。法伦警官站起身来伸了个懒腰说:"是基恩警官开着车回来了。现在,我们送你们几个回家。希望我们没有破坏您

85

的院子,利昂娜。"

"噢,别这么说。是你们保护了我的珠宝,还抓住了一对罪犯。"她说,"此外,我认识三个孩子,他们可能愿意通过耙草、种草这些劳动来赚些零花钱。"

法伦警官哈哈大笑起来:"看来您一个人就能抓住弗雷德·利特尔。您那把刀是从哪儿来的,利昂娜?"

"是在一次旅行中,我丈夫买回来的。"她微笑着说,"它在我床底下已经放了好些年,以防哪天我需要它。"

"您看到那家伙的脸了吗?"乔希问,"我觉得他会很高兴坐牢的。"

法伦警官和基恩警官把孩子们送到丁丁家。"晚安,孩子们。"法伦警官说,"别再在这附近偷偷摸摸地转悠了,好吗?"

孩子们答应会立刻上床睡觉,然后看着巡逻警车开走了。

"关于泰格,我怀疑弗雷德·利特尔说的不

是真话。"露丝说,"除了我的宠物,其他宠物都被送回去了。"

"明天我们会去帮你找找。对吗,乔希?"丁丁说。

"对的。"乔希说,"如果有必要,我们会按响绿地镇每户人家的门铃。"

露丝点了点头,看上去有点难过:"谢谢了,伙伴们。"

两个男孩跟露丝道了晚安,随后绕到屋子后面钻进了他们的帐篷。

乔希在黑暗中咯咯地笑:"你看见戴维斯太太脸上黏糊糊的就冲出家门的样子了吗?我还以为她是幽灵呢!"

丁丁咧着嘴笑了:"是的。弗雷德·利特尔像火箭一样从窗户里蹿了出来,我敢打赌,他从绳子上滑下来时两只手都磨伤了。"

丁丁翻了个身,闭上了眼睛。

三十秒后,露丝掀开帐篷的门帘,闯了进来,并用手电筒照向丁丁的脸。

"伙伴们,醒醒吧!"她大声叫道。

A to Z 神秘案件

乔希一骨碌爬起来:"天哪,露丝,我的小心脏今晚再也经不起任何惊吓了。"

"出什么事了?"丁丁一边问,一边眨巴着眼睛。

"泰格回家了!"露丝说着,扑通一声坐在丁丁的脚边,"我悄悄上楼时它就坐在我的床上呢。当我过去抱它的时候,它跳下床,钻到床底下去了。"

露丝咧着嘴笑了:"你们猜猜,除了泰格,我在床底下还发现了什么?"

"一把刀吗?"丁丁猜测道。

"不对!"

"一个入室窃贼吗?"乔希问道,在手电筒的光照下眨巴着眼睛。

"不!我发现了三只小猫咪。我当'外婆'啦!"

A to Z Mysteries®

THE CANARY CAPER

by Ron Roy

**illustrated by
John Steven Gurney**

INDIAN RIVER
LAWRENCE TAXI
RIVER ROAD
HORSE TRAILS
HORSES FOR RENT
BIKE PATH
WOODS
WOODVIEW ROAD
INDIAN WAY ROAD
FIRE STATION
BIKE PATH
BILL'S BIKES
SUPER MARKET
BRIDGE LANE
ROBIN ROAD
CROW ST
FINCH LA
THRUSH CT
OWL RD
PHEASANT LA
BLUE JAY WAY
WREN DR
FITNESS CENTER
WOODS
BIKE PATH
BLUE BIRD WAY
HUMMINGBIRD LA
WOODCOCK CROSS
ELLIE'S DINER
ACORN APTS
FURRY FEET PET SHOP
OAK STREET
BIKE PATH
CENTER CHURCH
PEOPLE'S POND
POST OFFICE
COMMUNITY GARDEN AND FISH POND
GREEN LAWN $ SAVINGS $ BANK
GOOSE ISLAND
RIVER ROAD
POLICE STATION
ELDERLY HOUSING
WEST GREEN ST
MAIN STREET
GREEN LAWN LIBRARY
SENIOR COMMUNITY CENTER
TOWN HALL
BIKE PATH
CHILDREN'S PETTING ZOO AND AQUARIUM
SHANGRI-LA HOTEL

WELCOME TO
GREEN LAWN
HOME OF THE
A to Z Mysteries
N
W
E
S
RIVER ROAD
BOAT LAUNCH
SQUAW ISLAND
GREEN LAWN MIDDLE SCHOOL
BOAT RENTAL
RON'S BAIT
DUCK WALK WAY
FARM LANE
JOSH
EAGLE LANE
MEADOW ROAD
GREEN LAWN ELEMENTARY SCHOOL
DINK
RUTH ROSE
TREE TOP CIRCLE
FOX LANE
QUAIL RUN ROAD
SILVER CIRCLE
WOODY STREET
BAND SHELL
ROSE GARDEN
PLEASANT STREET
THISTLE COURT
WILDFLOWER WAY
ROSE STREET
CENTER PARK
SWAN POND
GREEN LAWN HIGH SCHOOL
PLAYING FIELDS
GYM + POOL
BOXWOOD LANE
HOWARD'S BARBER-SHOP
BOOK NOOK
GAS STATION
CRYSTAL POND
MYSTIC GREENHOUSE
DOG KENNEL + VETERINARIAN
RIVER ROAD
EAST GREEN STREET
TOWN TENNIS COURTS
TOWN SWIMMING POOL
KIDDIE POOL
TOWN BASEBALL FIELD
TO THE BLUE HILLS

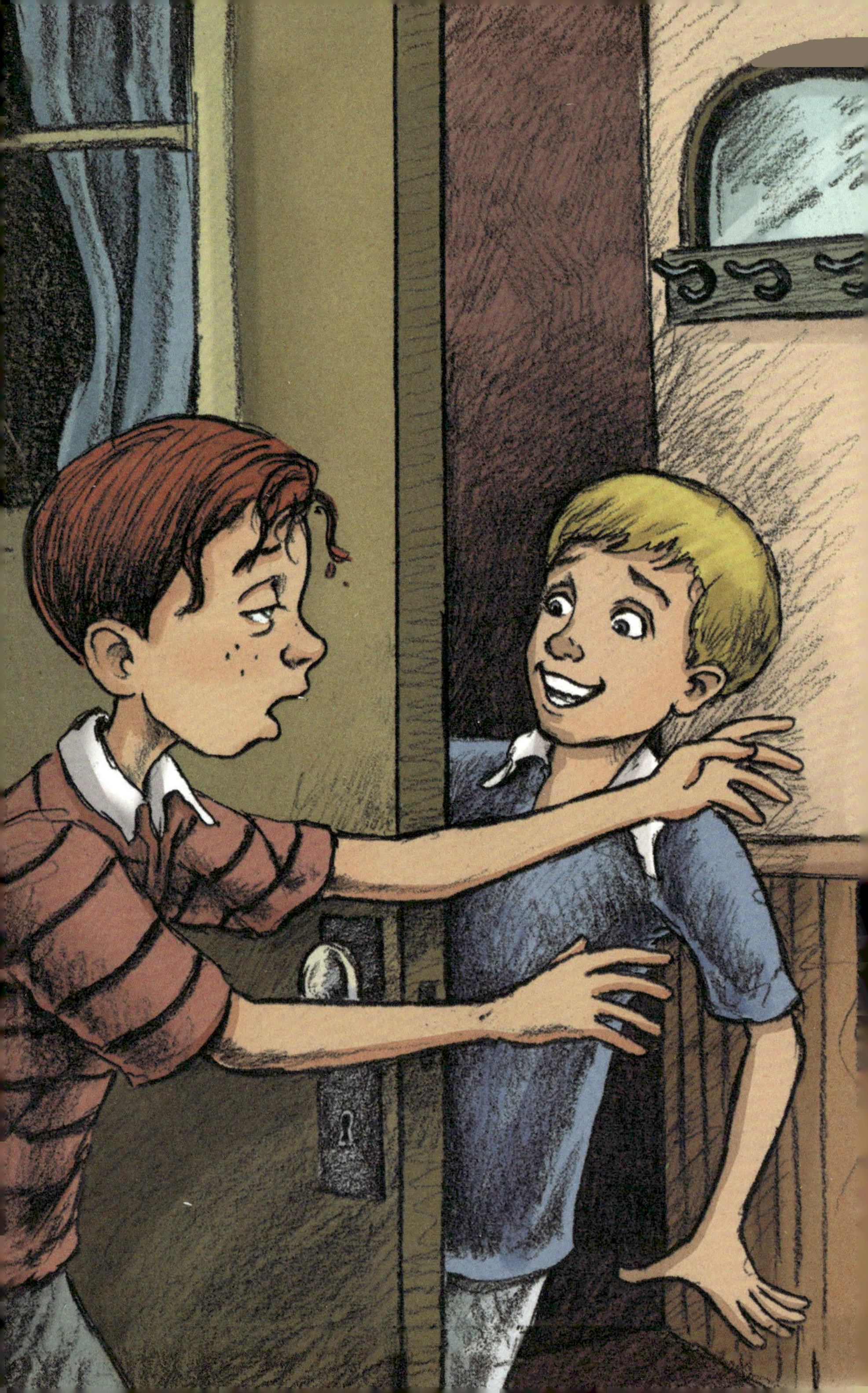

Chapter 1

Dink Duncan opened his front door. His best friend, Josh Pinto, was standing on the steps. "Hi, Josh. C'mon in," said Dink. "I just finished lunch."

Josh hurried past Dink, wiping his forehead. "We sure picked the hottest day of the summer to go to the circus," he said. "I just took a shower, and I'm still hot."

Dink grinned. "You took a shower? Let's see, that's

two showers this month, right?"

"Haw haw, very funny," Josh said. He opened the refrigerator door and pulled up his shirt. "Ahh, that feels good!"

"It won't feel so good if my mom catches you," Dink said.

Josh grabbed the apple juice and flopped into a chair. "You're funny, but it's too hot to laugh," he said, pouring himself a glass. "Where's Ruth Rose? It's almost time to leave."

"She's waiting next door." Dink put his plate in the sink. "I have to run up and brush my teeth."

"Forget your teeth—the circus is waiting!"

Dink grinned and pointed to a clown-faced cookie jar on the counter. "Grab a cookie. I'll be right down."

Josh made a beeline for the cookie jar. "Take your time brushing," he said.

"Don't eat all of them!" Dink said, leaping up the stairs.

"Dink," his mother called, "are you running?"

"Sorry, Mom," he called back. "We're in a hurry. Thursday is half-price admission if we get to the circus by one o'clock."

Dink brushed his teeth, yanked a comb through his blond hair, then charged back down the stairs.

"Donald David Duncan!" his mother yelled. "No running in the house!"

The phone rang in the kitchen.

"Got it, Mom!" Dink grabbed the phone, watching Josh stuff a whole cookie into his mouth. "Hello, Duncan residence."

Dink listened, then said, "We'll be over in five minutes." He hung up.

"We'll be over where in five minutes?" Josh asked.

"Mrs. Davis's house. You know her canary, Mozart? He's escaped."

"What about the circus?" asked Josh. "Half-price, remember?"

Dink shrugged. "So we pay full price. Mrs. Davis needs our help."

They walked next door to Ruth Rose's house and rang the bell. Four-year-old Nate Hathaway opened the door. He stared up at Dink with huge blue eyes.

"Hi, Natie," said Dink. "Is Ruth Rose ready?"

Nate's lips, cheeks, and T-shirt were smeared with chocolate. He was holding a raggedy stuffed dinosaur.

"Sheef ungt fruz," Nate said with a full mouth.

Dink laughed. "She's what?"

Ruth Rose showed up behind Nate. "MOM, WE'RE LEAVING NOW!" she screamed into the house.

Josh clapped both hands over his ears. "Ruth Rose, you should get a job as a car salesman. Then you could yell all day and get paid for it."

Ruth Rose stepped outside and closed the door. "You know perfectly well that I'm going to be President," she said sweetly. "And it's saleswoman, Josh."

Ruth Rose liked to dress in one color. Today it was purple, from her sneakers to the headband holding back her black curls.

While they walked down Woody Street, Dink told Ruth Rose about Mrs. Davis's missing canary.

"Mozart got out of his cage?" Ruth Rose said. "I hope he doesn't fly over here. Tiger could swallow a canary in one bite."

"Your fat cat could swallow a turkey in one bite,"

Josh said.

Ruth Rose rolled her eyes. "Tiger is plump," she said, "not fat. Race you!"

Mrs. Davis was standing in the doorway of her large yellow house when they arrived. "Thank you for coming right over," she said.

Mrs. Davis held a handkerchief, and her eyes were red. "I didn't know who else to call."

"We don't mind," Dink said. "What happened to Mozart?"

"After breakfast, I hung his cage outback so he could have some fresh air. But when I went to give him his lunch, his cage was empty!"

"I'm sure he's somewhere nearby. Don't worry!" Dink said.

Dink, Josh, and Ruth Rose ran around to the backyard. Mozart's cage was hanging in an apple tree.

"Split up," Dink said. "Check all the bushes and flowers."

The kids searched every tree, shrub, and flower bed. Mrs. Davis watched from her back porch. "Any luck?" she asked Dink.

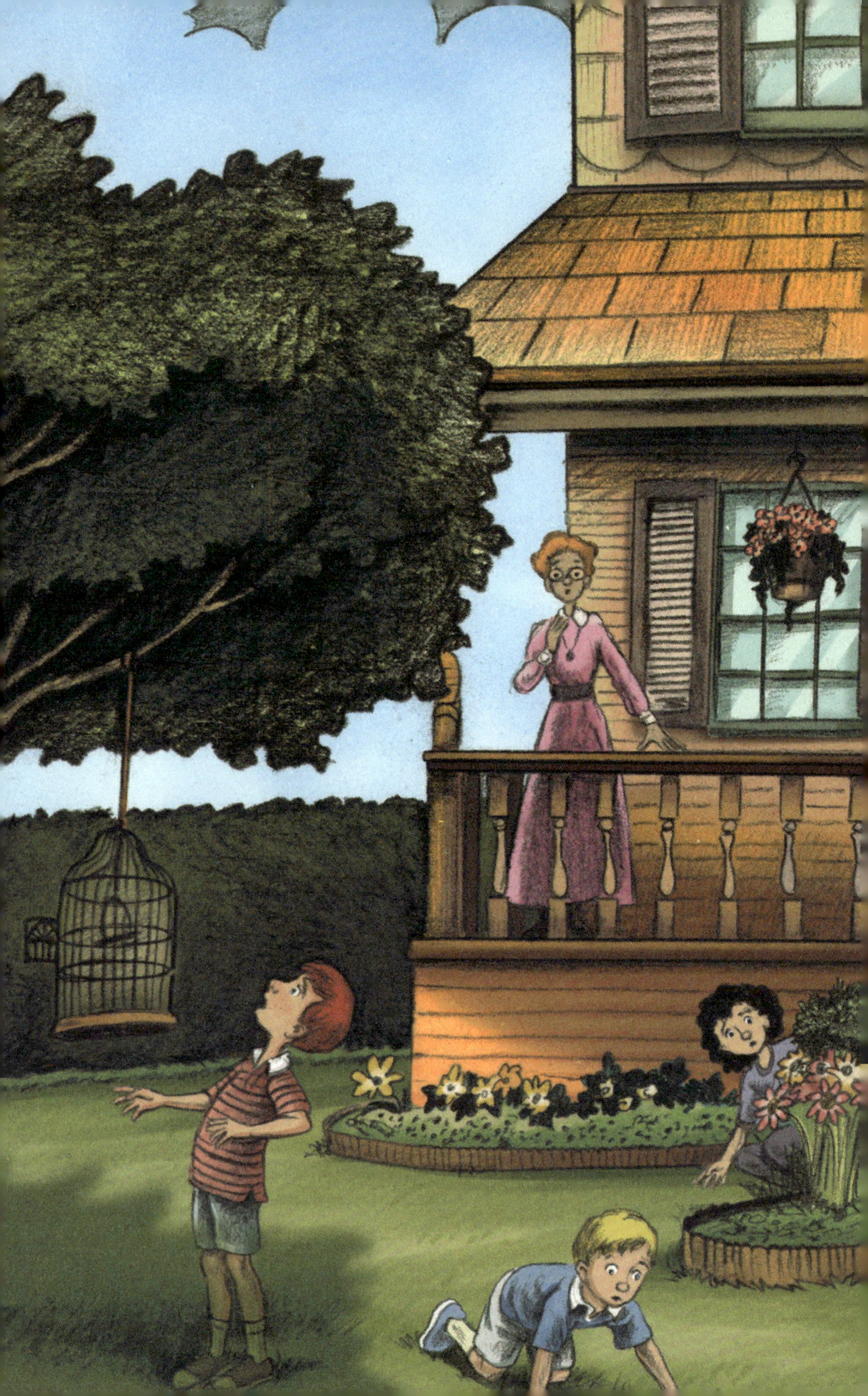

He shook his head. "I'm afraid not, but we'll keep looking."

"It's such a beautiful day," Mrs. Davis said. "I hope you kids have something fun planned."

"After we find Mozart, we're going to the circus," Dink told her.

"The circus! Well, please don't let me stop you!" Mrs. Davis said. "Mozart knows his cage. I'm sure he'll fly home soon."

But Dink could tell that Mrs. Davis wasn't really so sure. "Okay, but we'll call you later," he promised.

They said good-bye to Mrs. Davis and headed for the high school. The Tinker Town Traveling Circus had set up on the school baseball field the day before and would leave town Monday night.

The kids cut through a bunch of circus trailers and trucks on their way to the admissions gate. The sides of the trailers were painted with pictures of clowns, tigers, and elephants.

They arrived five minutes after one, but the ticket lady let them in for half-price anyway, a dollar each.

"What'll we do first?" Ruth Rose asked.

"Let's eat," Josh said.

"No way," Dink said. "You already had lunch, and you probably gobbled down half my mom's cookies. Let's walk around and see what's here."

They watched birds do tricks, dogs ride on

ponies, and a chimp dressed like Elvis "sing" into a microphone.

They all gulped when a tiger trainer put his hand right inside a tiger's mouth.

"Guess the tiger's not hungry," Josh said with a

grin.

In Clown Corner, a clown dressed as a giraffe danced on stilts. He kept time to the music by snapping his yellow suspenders.

"I have to leave soon," Ruth Rose said after a while. "My mom needs me to watch Nate while she goes shopping."

The kids left, cutting through the town rose garden to get to Woody Street.

Dink snapped his fingers. "I just remembered—my mom said I can set up my tent in the backyard. Can you guys get permission to sleep out?"

"No problem for me," Josh said.

"Nate's never slept in a tent, so I'll bring him," Ruth Rose said. "And Tiger," she added sweetly.

"Your little brother!" Josh yelped. "Great, we'll have our own circus—a four-year-old monkey and a man-eating tiger!"

Ruth Rose laughed. "Don't worry. We'll bring our own tent."

Dink and Josh dropped Ruth Rose off at her house, then continued on to Dink's. There they went inside and called Mrs. Davis.

"She says Mozart hasn't come back," Dink told Josh after he'd hung up.

While they were pitching Dink's tent, Ruth Rose came over. Nate trailed behind her, dragging his extinct-looking stuffed dinosaur.

"Hey, where's your man-eating cat?" Josh asked.

Ruth Rose dropped her tent on the ground. She looked as if she'd just swallowed something nasty.

"What's the matter, Ruth Rose?" Dink asked.

"Tiger is missing," Ruth Rose said quietly. "And my mother says she hasn't been home all day."

Chapter 2

Early the next morning, Ruth Rose poked her head into Dink's tent. "Wake up, you guys!"

Dink shot up out of a sound sleep. "Did Tiger come back?" he asked, peering sleepily at Ruth Rose.

"No, she didn't. I'm going to the police station and I want you guys to come with me."

Josh rolled over in his sleeping bag. "To report a missing cat?"

"No, to report a missing cat and a missing canary,"

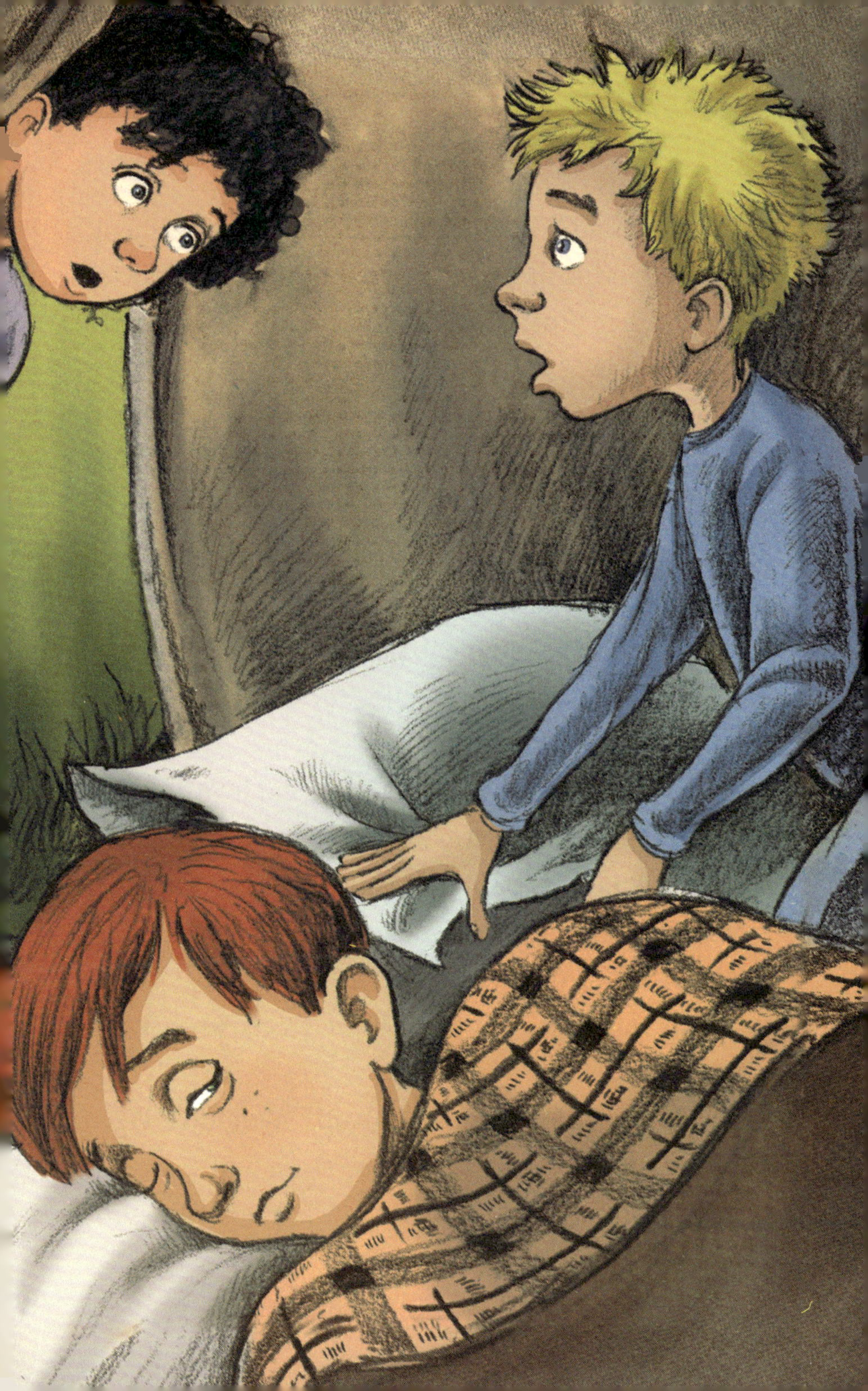

Ruth Rose said. Then she ducked back out of the tent.

Dink and Josh looked at each other, then crawled out after her. Ruth Rose was pacing back and forth across the lawn.

"Guys, it's just too weird," she said. "Two animals disappeared from the same street on the same day!" Ruth Rose stopped pacing and looked at them. "I don't think Mozart and Tiger wandered off, I think they were stolen. I'm taking Nate home, and then you guys are coming with me to talk to Officer Fallon."

Ruth Rose woke up Nate, took his hand, and marched toward her house.

Dink and Josh just looked at each other and shrugged. Then they walked into Dink's house. Josh poured two bowls of cereal while Dink ran up to his room to change. Loretta, his guinea pig, squeaked a hello to Dink from her cage.

Josh was slurping up his Weet Treets when Dink came back down.

"I've been thinking," Josh said. "Wouldn't Tiger eat Mozart if someone kidnapped them both?"

Dink shrugged. "I don't know. I'm not even sure

that Tiger and Mozart were kidnapped," he said between bites. "But Ruth Rose is our friend, so let's go to the police station with her."

Ruth Rose walked in wearing blue shorts and a red shirt. "You guys ready to go?" she asked.

Dink stared. He'd never seen Ruth Rose wear two different colors at the same time. He gave Josh a look, but Josh was busy reading the back of the cereal box and didn't notice.

"Yup, we're ready," Dink said, putting the bowls and glasses in the sink.

They found Officer Fallon at his desk. He was typing at his computer, chewing gum, and sipping tea all at the same time.

"Well, hi, gang," he said, smiling at the kids. "Going to the circus this weekend? How about some free passes?"

"No thanks, we went yesterday," Dink said.

Officer Fallon handed Josh three tickets. "Go again, on the Green Lawn Police!"

"Officer Fallon, I have a problem," Ruth Rose said.

He pointed at some chairs. "Have a seat. I'm all

ears."

"It's my cat, Tiger. She's been gone for a whole day and night," Ruth Rose said. "She's never been away from home that long! Mrs. Davis's canary disappeared, too!"

Dink had never seen Ruth Rose look or sound so serious.

Officer Fallon wrote something on a sheet of paper.

"I think someone in Green Lawn is stealing pets," Ruth Rose went on. "Two pets vanishing on the same day is just too weird!"

"Four pets," Officer Fallon said. He opened his drawer and pulled out a sheet of paper. "Four pets are missing."

"Four?" Dink and Josh said together.

Officer Fallon nodded. "Last night, Dr. Pardue called. His kids' rabbit was missing from its cage. Later, Mrs. Gwynn called. It seems her parrot disappeared off her back porch."

"All yesterday?" Dink asked.

Officer Fallon nodded.

"I was right!" Ruth Rose said, jumping to her feet. "There is a pet-napper around here!"

"Four animals disappearing on the same day does seem strange," Officer Fallon said. "In fact, I've already asked Officer Keene to look into it."

He looked at Ruth Rose. "Could it be that your cat just took a little vacation, Ruth Rose? I used to have a cat who was a real wanderer."

"Well, Tiger isn't," Ruth Rose answered firmly.

Officer Fallon nodded. He told the kids he'd let them know if he discovered anything.

The kids left the police station and walked toward Main Street.

"Sounds like you might be right, Ruth Rose," Dink said.

"Maybe we should go see Mrs. Wong, just in case," Josh suggested. "People always bring her stray animals. Maybe someone found Tiger and brought her to the pet shop."

Ruth Rose rewarded Josh with a huge smile. "Great idea, Josh!"

They passed Howard's Barbershop. Howard was

A to Z 神秘案件

out front, sweeping his sidewalk.

"Have you seen my big orange cat?" Ruth Rose called.

Howard shook his head. "Sorry, Ruth Rose."

At the Furry Feet pet shop, Mrs. Wong told Ruth Rose the same thing. "Nobody brought Tiger in," she said. "But I'll keep my eyes peeled."

"Mrs. Davis's canary is gone, too," Dink told Mrs. Wong.

"And Dr. Pardue's rabbit and Mrs. Gwynn's parrot!" Josh said.

"Four animals are missing? That is very strange!"

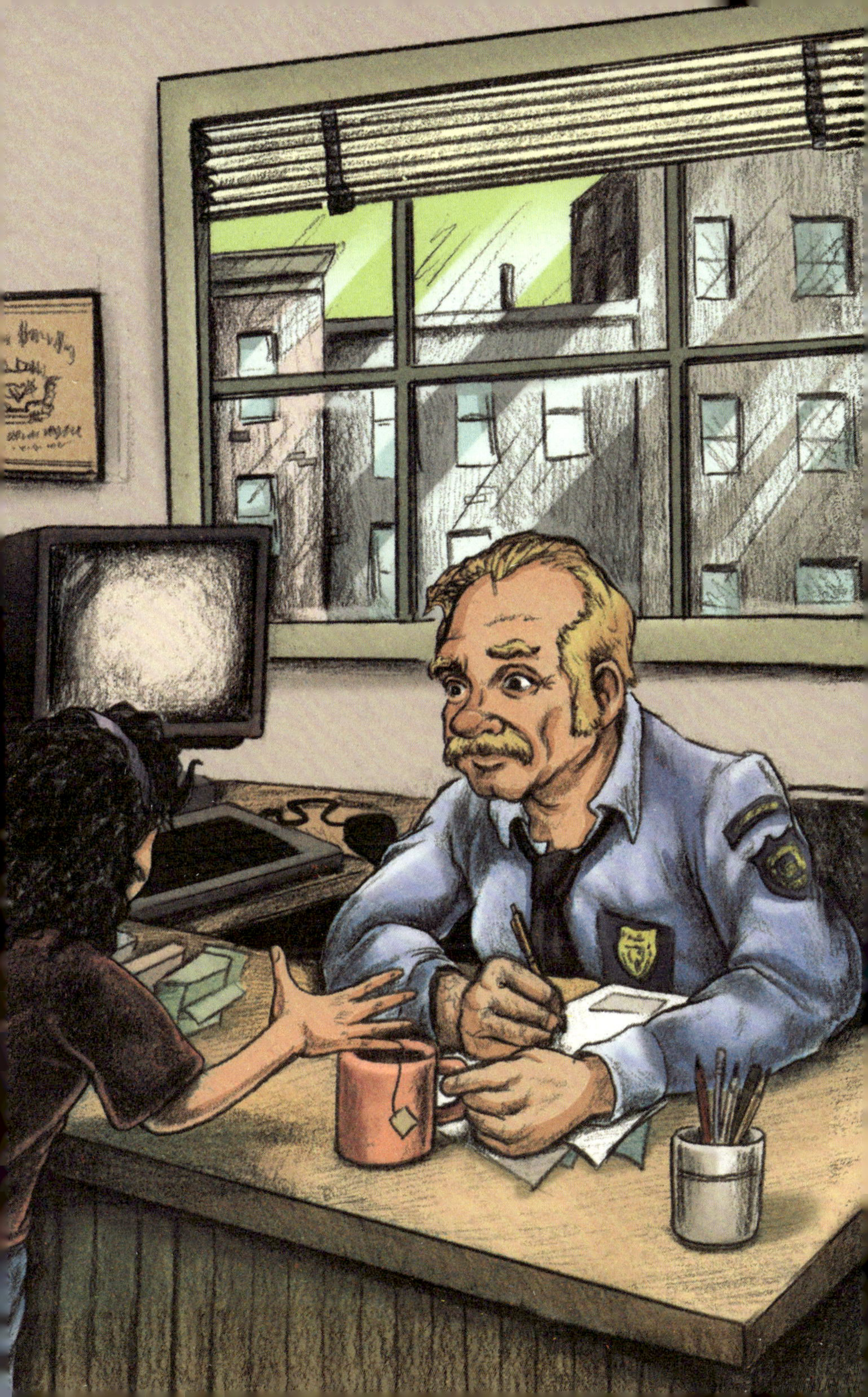

Mrs. Wong glanced around her shop. "I guess I should count my own critters!"

"May I use your phone, Mrs. Wong?" Ruth Rose asked. "I want to call my mom and see if Tiger's home yet."

"Help yourself," Mrs. Wong said.

Ruth Rose dialed, spoke quietly to her mother, then hung up.

"Tiger's still gone," she said. "Who'd want to steal a canary, a cat, a parrot, and a rabbit?"

"I don't know," Dink said. "But we're going to find out!"

Chapter 3

The kids left the pet shop and headed up Main Street. They walked slowly, thinking about what to do.

"I've read about scientists stealing animals to use in experiments," Josh said.

"That's awful!" Dink said.

"I don't want Tiger used in some experiment!" said Ruth Rose. "We have to find those animals. Where do the Gwynns and the Pardues live?"

"The Gwynns live over by us, on Thistle Court," Dink said.

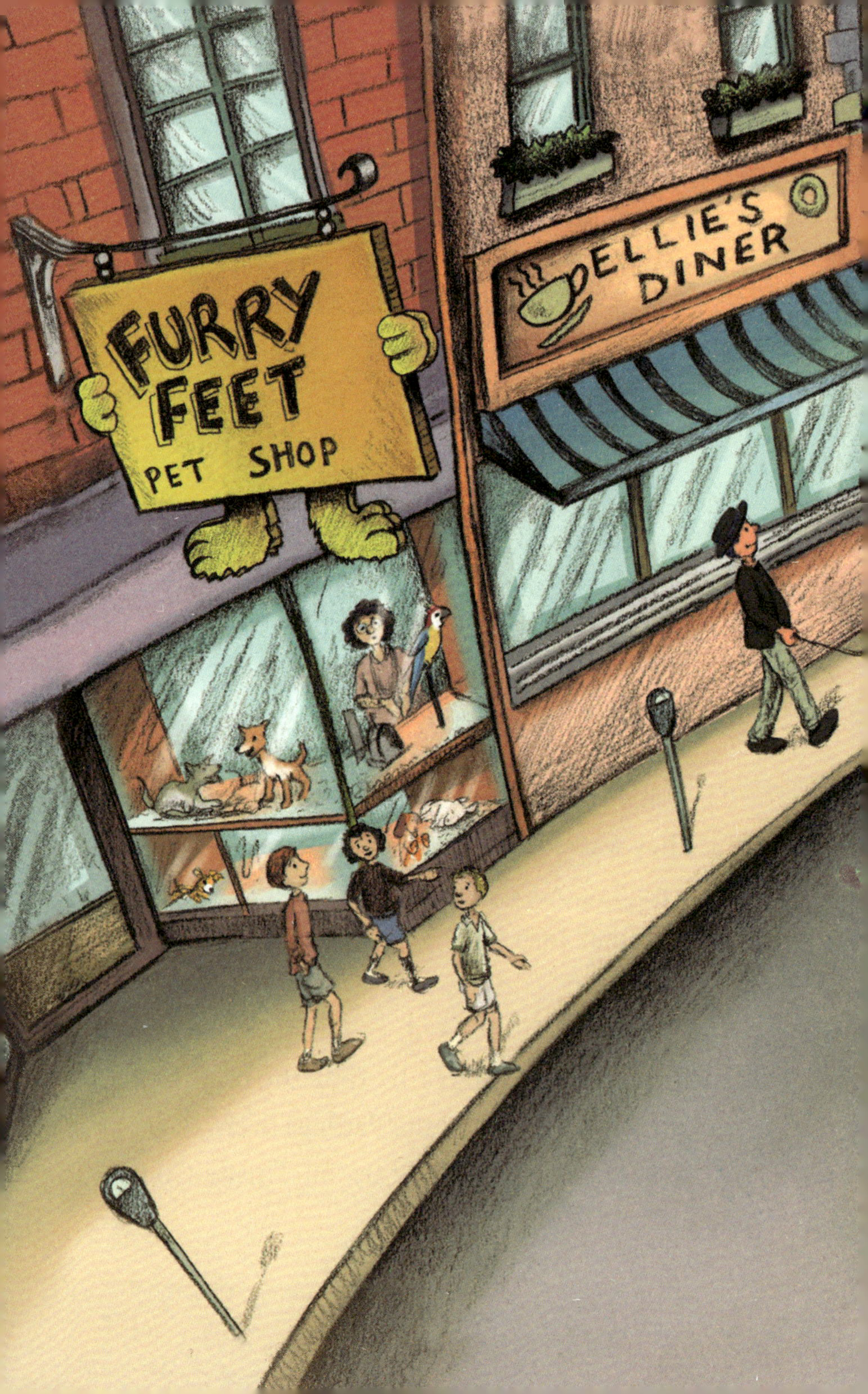
FURRY FEET
PET SHOP
ELLIE'S DINER

"Why don't we go talk to them?" Ruth Rose said. "Maybe the pet-napper left some clues."

The kids cut through the high school grounds and passed the circus trailers. A few of the workers were sitting at a picnic table drinking coffee. They waved when the kids walked by.

"Which house is the Gwynns'?" Ruth Rose asked when they reached Thistle Court.

"That big gray one," Josh said. The mailbox in

front said GWYNN in black letters.

Ruth Rose walked up the steps and rang the doorbell. Mrs. Gwynn opened the door.

"Hi, kids! How's your summer so far?" she asked.

"Not so great," Ruth Rose said. "Someone stole my cat yesterday."

"Oh, Ruth Rose, how awful! My parrot disappeared yesterday, too!"

"So did Mrs. Davis's canary," Josh added.

"We just came from the police station," Dink put in. "Officer Fallon told us about your parrot. Dr. Pardue's rabbit is also missing."

Mrs. Gwynn's mouth fell open. "My goodness! Do you mean that four pets disappeared yesterday?"

"We think so," Ruth Rose said. "Where was your parrot when you last saw him?"

"On my back porch, in his cage," Mrs. Gwynn said.

"Can we see the cage?" Dink asked.

Mrs. Gwynn took them through the kitchen to a screened-in back porch. A cage stood in one corner.

"Archie likes it out here," said Mrs. Gwynn. "He

can watch the other birds in the trees. Yesterday I came out to have my lunch, but he was gone."

Dink checked the screen door that led to the backyard. "Was this locked?" he asked.

"I don't really remember. We often leave it unlocked," Mrs. Gwynn said.

"Could Archie have opened his cage door himself?" Josh asked.

Mrs. Gwynn shook her head. "We always keep a clothespin on his door to make sure he can't open it."

"So someone must have stolen him," Ruth Rose said.

"Oh, dear, I don't like to think of crime in Green Lawn," Mrs. Gwynn said with a sigh. "Can I offer you kids something to drink? It's pretty warm."

"No thanks," Ruth Rose said. "But do you mind if we look in your phone book for Dr. Pardue's address?"

"They're at number three Pheasant Lane," Mrs. Gwynn said. "I drop Mike off there to play tennis with Andy Pardue."

The kids thanked Mrs. Gwynn and hurried to

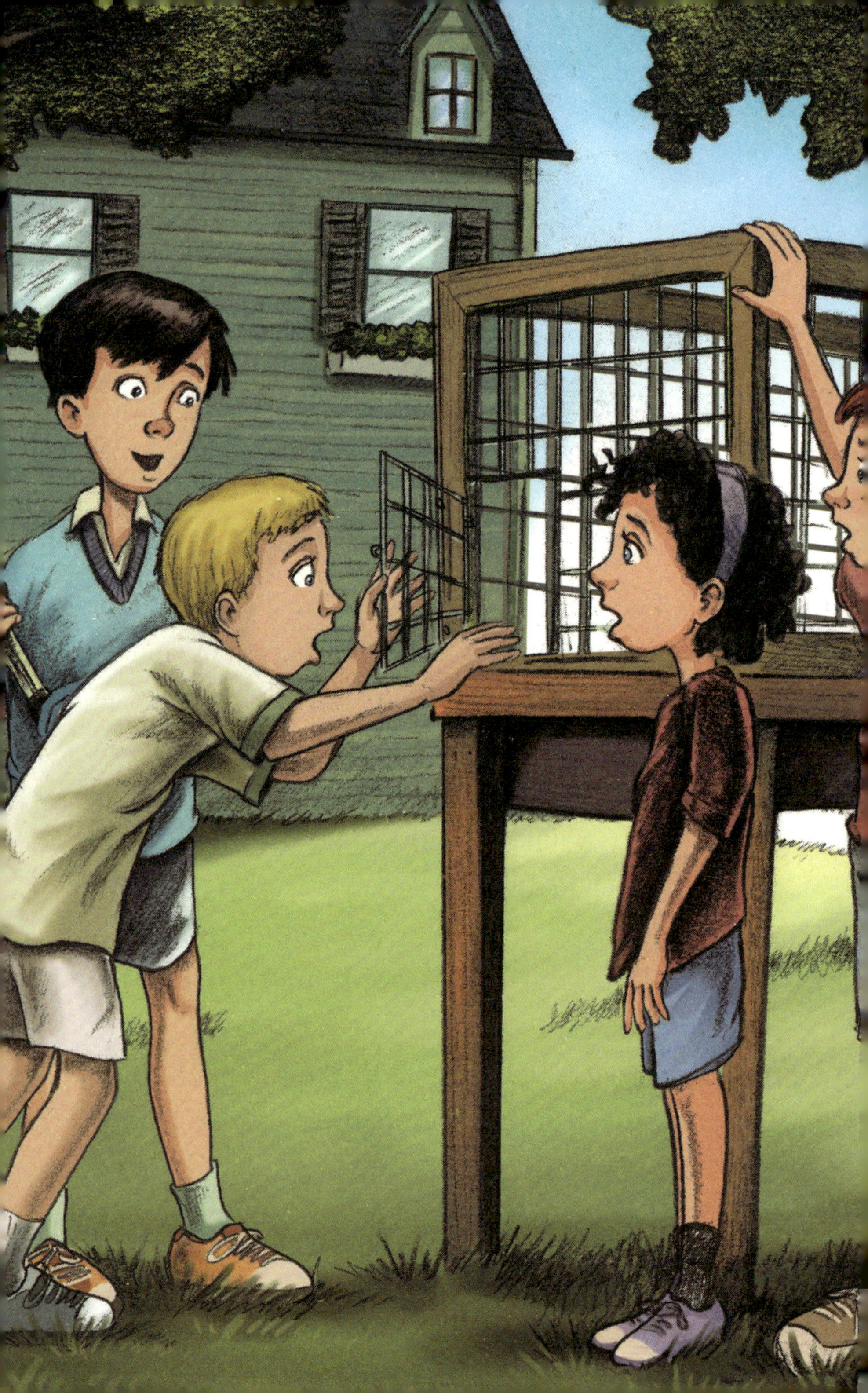

金丝雀之谜

Main Street.

"This is getting weirder and weirder," Dink said. "A canary and a parrot were snatched right out of their cages in broad daylight. With people home!"

"And Tiger was probably in my backyard when she was taken," Ruth Rose said.

They waved to Mr. Paskey at the Book Nook and headed up Aviary Way. Three Pheasant Lane was a big green house surrounded by tall trees. A kid holding a tennis racket was sitting on the front porch.

"Hi," Ruth Rose said, walking up to the porch. "Is Dr. Pardue home? We'd like to talk to him about his rabbit."

"I'm Andy Pardue," the kid said. "Violet's my rabbit. Why? Did you find her?"

"No, but my cat is missing, too," Ruth Rose said. "And so are two other pets in town."

Dink glanced around the Pardues' front yard. "When did your rabbit disappear?" he asked Andy.

"After lunch yesterday," he said. "My sister ran into the house screaming. I went out to the cage, and the door was wide open. Violet was gone."

121

"Can you show us the cage?" Ruth Rose asked.

Andy led them to the backyard. An empty rabbit hutch stood under a tree.

"Was the cage locked?" Josh asked.

"Yep, I lock it every night myself." Andy Pardue gave them a sharp look. "What's going on, anyway? A ring of animal thieves?"

"That's what we're trying to find out," Dink said.

"Well, let me know what you dig up," said Andy. "Boy, I'd like to get my hands on the creep who did this. My little sister cried all night!"

The kids walked back to Woody Street.

"Let's stop and check in with Mrs. Davis," Dink suggested as they passed her house. "We should tell her about the other missing animals."

When Mrs. Davis opened her door, she had a big smile on her face.

"Oh, I'm so glad to see you three!" she exclaimed. "You'll never guess! A man just called. He said he found Mozart! He's bringing him here at six-thirty. Isn't that lovely?"

"That's great." Dink looked at Josh and Ruth Rose

in surprise.

"I want you three to be here, since you were kind enough to look for him," Mrs. Davis continued. "Afterward, we'll have some of my strawberry shortcake to celebrate!"

"Super!" Josh said.

"We'll see you at six-thirty," Dink said with a wave. The three started home.

Josh grinned. "I guess Mozart wasn't kidnapped after all."

"I guess not," Dink said. He looked at Ruth Rose. She wasn't smiling.

"There's one thing I don't understand," she finally said. "How did he know who to call? How did that man know who Mozart belonged to?"

Dink shrugged. "Maybe he found him near Mrs. Davis's house and asked one of her neighbors."

"Or," Ruth Rose said, "maybe the guy who called is the same guy who took Mozart."

"But that doesn't make sense," Dink said. "Why would someone steal a canary on Thursday and return it the next day?"

"For the reward," Ruth Rose said with a frown. "This guy steals pets, then returns them for money."

Dink and Josh just stared at Ruth Rose.

They walked the rest of the way home in silence.

Chapter 4

Dink and Ruth Rose sat on Dink's front porch. They'd just finished dinner and were waiting for Josh.

Ruth Rose sighed.

"Tiger hasn't come home yet?" Dink asked.

She shook her head.

"Cats can be pretty mysterious sometimes," Dink said. He wanted Ruth Rose to feel better. "Maybe she's visiting a cat buddy somewhere."

Ruth Rose looked down. "She's never stayed away like this."

Suddenly Dink noticed that Ruth Rose had forgotten

her headband. Her curly hair was hanging in her eyes.

Just then Josh came running down Woody Street, carrying his sketch pad. He jogged across Dink's lawn.

"Did Tiger come back yet?" he asked.

"No," Ruth Rose said, standing up. "Come on, let's go see who brings Mozart back."

A few minutes later, they were ringing Mrs. Davis's doorbell. Ruth Rose had a determined look in her eye. "If this guy has cat scratches on his hands, I'm calling Officer Fallon."

Mrs. Davis opened her door dressed for the occasion. The green gem in her necklace sparkled in the evening sunlight.

"I hope you've brought your appetites," she said. "To help us celebrate Mozart's return, I've made some shortcake."

Josh grinned. "I might be able to eat a small helping."

Mrs. Davis laughed. "Oh, pooh, Joshua Pinto. I've seen what you can do to a batch of my cookies."

They walked into the living room. Mozart's empty cage sat on the piano.

"It will be so good to hear Mozart sing again," Mrs. Davis said.

The doorbell chimed. "He's here!" Mrs. Davis hurried to the door.

A thin young man stood smiling on the front porch. He was dressed neatly in a white shirt, dark pants, and blue suspenders.

The man held a small box with holes poked in the sides. "I'm Fred Little," he said. "Here's your canary."

Dink looked at the man's hands as he passed the box to Mrs. Davis. Not a single claw mark. He shot a look at Ruth Rose.

"Thank you, Mr. Little," said Mrs. Davis. "Won't you step inside?"

Mrs. Davis introduced him to Dink Josh, and Ruth Rose. Then she opened the box and lifted out her canary.

"Well, Mozart, how was your vacation?" She gave the canary a quick kiss and placed him in his cage.

Everyone paused to watch Mozart hop around, then settle down to preen his feathers.

"Mr. Little, I can't tell you how grateful I am," Mrs.

Davis said. "But how did you know where to bring him?"

Ruth Rose kicked Dink in the ankle.

Fred Little smiled. "I had to do some detective work," he said. "I called the pet shop today and asked who in town owned a canary. A nice woman told me your name, so I looked you up in the phone book."

"That must have been Mrs. Wong," Dink said. "We talked to her today, too. About Ruth Rose's missing cat. When did you call her?"

The man stared at Dink. "I don't remember exactly," he said. "It was right after I caught the canary."

Mrs. Davis clapped her hands. "How thoughtful of you to go to so much trouble! Will you accept a reward?"

Ruth Rose glanced at Dink with a smirk on her

face.

The man smiled at Mrs. Davis. "You're very kind," he said. "But no thanks. It's reward enough seeing your little bird back home again."

Dink snuck a quick look at Ruth Rose. She looked confused, and Dink could understand why.

If he won't take a reward, then he didn't steal Mozart. And if Mozart didn't get kidnapped, maybe Tiger didn't either, Dink thought.

"Then will you at least have a cup of tea and a cookie?" Mrs. Davis asked.

"That'll be fine," he said. "May I use your bathroom?"

"Down the hall on the right," Mrs. Davis said. "Kids, will you help me in the kitchen?"

While Mrs. Davis boiled water and arranged her silver tea service, the kids put cookies on a tray.

"He didn't take the reward," Ruth Rose whispered, frowning. "I can't believe I was wrong!"

"I don't know, Ruth Rose," Dink said. "There's something fishy about this guy. Why didn't Mrs. Wong tell us he called her?"

"We saw Mrs. Wong in the morning," Josh reminded them. "Fred Little must have called her later."

"Yeah, I suppose," Dink said.

"But I have this weird feeling I've seen Fred Little somewhere before," Josh said.

"Around here?" Ruth Rose asked.

Josh shrugged. "I'm not sure. I can't remember."

"What are you three whispering about?" Mrs. Davis called. "I'll need some helping hands in a minute."

When they were all seated around the card table, Mrs. Davis poured five cups of tea. "Are you just passing through, Mr. Little? I haven't seen you in town before."

"I'm here looking for a job," Fred Little said.

"So you might settle in Green Lawn? Wouldn't that be wonderful!"

Fred Little smiled. "It's a nice town." He glanced around the living room. "You sure have a lovely home, Mrs. Davis."

"Why, thank you. When my husband was alive, we traveled a great deal," Mrs. Davis said. "We brought back something special from each country we visited."

Fred Little left a few minutes later, and the kids helped Mrs. Davis clean up. "Still have room for shortcake?" she asked, grinning at Josh.

"Sure do!" he answered, picking up his sketch pad.

Josh began to draw a picture of Fred Little's face. "I just wish I could remember where I've seen this guy before."

Chapter 5

That night, a thunderstorm sent the kids running from their tents into their houses.

It was still raining the next day, so they decided to play Monopoly at Dink's house.

"Ruth Rose, it's your turn," Josh said.

"I know," she said, staring out Dink's window. "I can't concentrate. Tiger is out there in the rain."

Dink and Josh just looked at each other.

"If Fred Little didn't take the pets, then who could it be?" Ruth Rose asked. She came and plopped herself down at the Monopoly board.

Dink thought a moment. "If we could figure out why someone was stealing animals," he said, "maybe we could figure out who was doing it."

Ruth Rose picked up her stack of Monopoly cash. "I still think it's for money," she said. "When people get kidnapped, it's usually for ransom money, right?"

The boys nodded.

"But no one who's lost a pet has gotten a ransom note," Josh said.

"Not yet, anyway." Ruth Rose tossed her play money onto the table. "I'm going home. Mom put an ad in the paper, and I want to be there if anyone calls about Tiger."

The two boys watched her put on her coat and head out into the rain.

"I've never seen her act so mopey," Josh said after the door closed. "She doesn't even argue with me anymore!"

"Yeah, and have you noticed she's not wearing one color either?" Dink pointed out. "I hope Tiger comes home soon."

That night the rain cleared up, so Dink and Josh

slept out in the tent again.

The next morning, Ruth Rose woke them up. She was wearing cut-off jeans and an old T-shirt. Her untied sneaker laces were muddy from dragging.

"Read this, guys," she said, and she shoved the Sunday Morning Gazette under Dink's nose.

One paragraph was circled in red crayon. Dink and Josh stumbled out of the tent and sat at the picnic table.

The paragraph was under LOCAL AREA CRIMES. Dink scanned it quickly, then read it out loud:

"Two Green Lawn homes were burglarized last night, Officer Charles Fallon has reported. The homes of Dr. and Mrs. Michael Pardue and Mr. and Mrs. Harvey Gwynn were entered by persons unknown. Several items of value were taken. Police are investigating."

Dink looked up. "Wow! First they lose their pets, then someone breaks into their houses. I think that stinks!"

"And I think they're connected," Ruth Rose said. "Don't you see, it is about money! Someone is taking pets, then breaking into the same houses."

"But why would someone need to steal a pet before robbing a house?" Dink asked.

"And not only that," Josh added, "but what about you and Mrs. Davis? Your pets disappeared, but your houses weren't broken into."

"He's right, Ruth Rose," Dink said. "Why just two houses and not all four?"

Ruth Rose frowned at Dink and Josh. "I don't know," she said.

"We should try and find out. Let's go see the Pardues and the Gwynns again. Maybe the burglars left some clues!"

They hurried over to Thistle Court and rang the bell. Mr. Gwynn came to the door in his bathrobe.

"Oh, hi, kids! Mrs. Gwynn told me you stopped by Friday. Guess what? Yesterday afternoon, someone found our parrot and returned him!"

Ruth Rose stared at Mr. Gwynn. "Archie was returned yesterday?"

Mr. Gwynn nodded. "To celebrate, I took the family out for dinner and a movie. But when we got

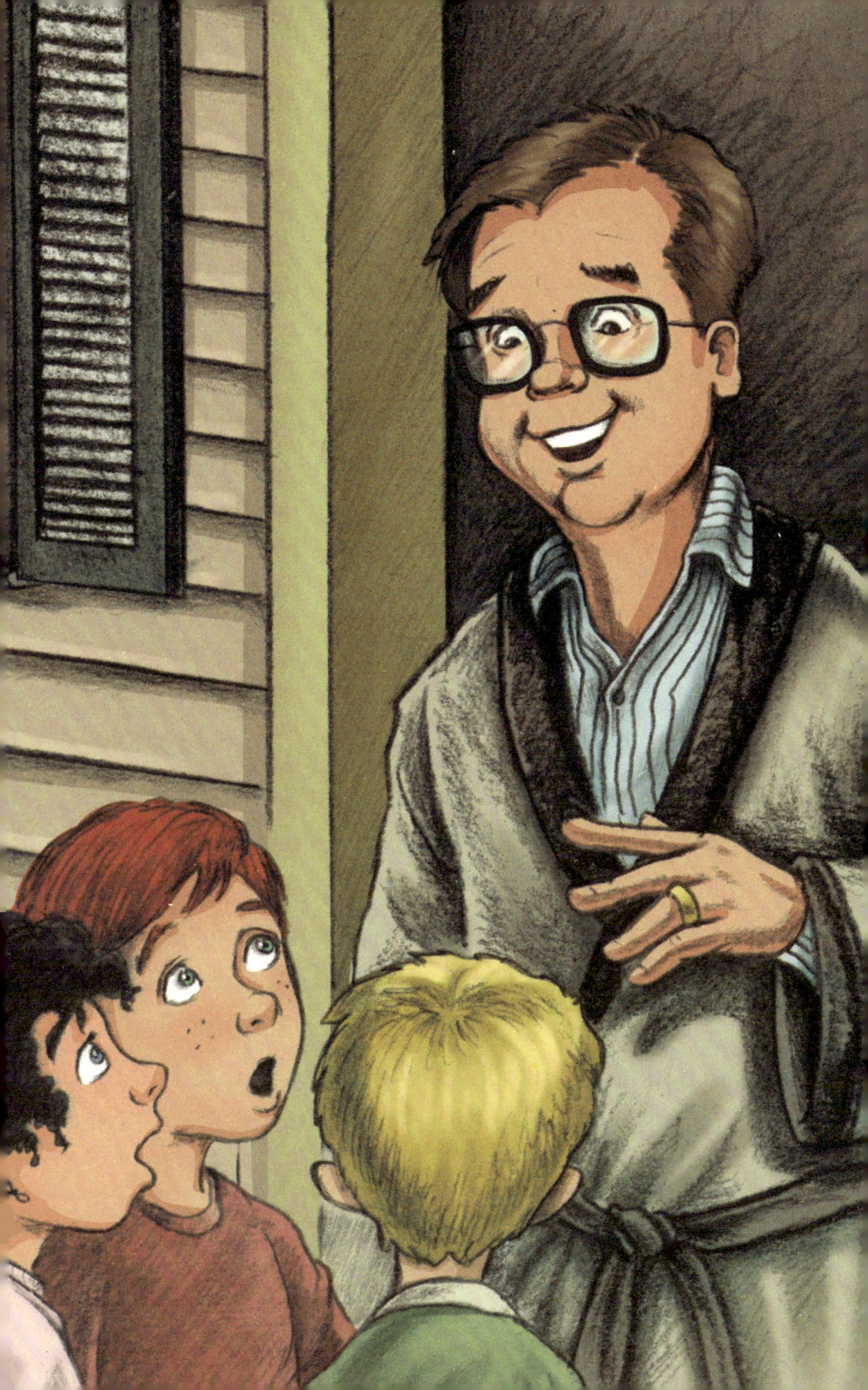

back home, we discovered we'd been robbed. The rats took my coin collection."

"I'm sorry to hear that," Dink said.

"May I ask who returned your parrot?"

"A nice young woman," Mr. Gwynn told the kids. "She said she'd caught Archie eating seeds under her bird feeder."

"Did you invite her into your house?" Ruth Rose asked.

Before he could answer, Dink blurted out, "Did she see your coin collection?"

Mr. Gwynn's mouth dropped open. "Are you suggesting…Oh, my, you could be right!" he said. "The collection was in the living room where we sat and talked. Do you think she came back and stole it?"

Dink, Josh, and Ruth Rose looked at one another. Ruth Rose had her "I told you so!" look on her face.

"It sure seems that way, Mr. Gwynn," Dink said.

The kids thanked Mr. Gwynn, then raced all the way to the Pardues' house. Out of breath, Ruth Rose rang the bell.

Mrs. Pardue came to the door. "Hi, gang, what's

up?" she said.

Ruth Rose asked, "By any chance, did someone bring your rabbit back yesterday, before your house got robbed?"

"Why, how did you know?" Mrs. Pardue asked. "A nice young couple called and said they'd found Violet in their garden. They brought her home yesterday afternoon."

Dink explained how the Gwynns' parrot had also been returned before they were robbed.

Mrs. Pardue's eyes got wide. "Of course! That couple came in and had a cold drink with us. Dr. Pardue offered them a reward, but they refused it."

"What did they steal?" Josh asked.

"Several pieces of my good jewelry," Mrs. Pardue said. "Some of it was left to me by my grandmother."

Ruth Rose thought for a minute. "Did they ask to use your bathroom?"

"Yes, the woman did," Mrs. Pardue answered. "She could have snooped in my bedroom at the same time. I feel so foolish!"

The kids said good-bye and headed for Main

Street.

"I knew it!" Ruth Rose said. "The pet-nappers and the robbers are the same people!"

"Boy, what a dirty scam," Josh said. "You steal someone's pet, return it to get a guided tour of the place, then come back later to take what you liked."

"Talk about a double whammy," Dink said, shaking his head.

"I think it's gonna be a triple whammy," Ruth Rose said. "What about Mrs. Davis?"

"What about her?" Josh asked. "She hasn't…oh, my gosh!"

"That's right," Ruth Rose said. "I'll bet anything that Mrs. Davis's house is next!"

Chapter 6

"Or your house could be next," Dink reminded Ruth Rose.

Ruth Rose shook her head. "They didn't return Tiger, so they didn't get inside my house. Come on, we have to tell Officer Fallon!"

They ran down Main Street to the police station.

"Does he work on Sunday morning?" Josh asked as they hurried up the steps.

"We'll find out in a minute," Dink said.

The kids almost bumped into Officer Fallon coming through the door.

"Were you kids coming to see me?" he asked. "I was just heading for Ellie's."

"Officer Fallon, we figured out the burglaries!" Ruth Rose cried.

He looked at her. "Oh? Then we'd better go back inside."

Sitting at his desk, Officer Fallon picked up a pencil. "I'm listening," he said.

Ruth Rose told him their theory about how the pet-nappers came back later to return the animals, then rob the houses.

Officer Fallon smiled. "I think you're right on the button," he said. "I figured out the same thing."

"Did you know that Mrs. Davis's canary was returned, too?" Ruth Rose asked. She looked at Dink and Josh. "We think her house will be robbed next!"

Officer Fallon raised his eyebrows. "Well, now, that is news. I didn't know about the canary. When was it returned?" he asked, writing something on his pad.

"Friday night," Josh said. "Some guy called up and said he'd found Mozart. He brought him over while we were there."

Officer Fallon's eyes widened. "Tell me about this man, Josh," he said quietly.

Josh described Fred Little while Officer Fallon took more notes.

"Can you arrest Fred Little before he breaks into Mrs. Davis's house?" Ruth Rose asked.

Officer Fallon tapped his pencil and squinted one eye at the kids. "Officer Keene and I have been looking for whoever returned the Gywnn and Pardue pets. We want to question them about the petnappings and the robberies. Now we will start looking for Fred Little, too."

He leaned forward on his elbows. "But we have no evidence that these people have done anything wrong. The same goes for Fred Little. True, here turned the canary and got inside Leona Davis's house. That's the same pattern as the other two burglaries, but it's not a crime."

"You can't arrest him?" Josh asked.

Officer Fallon shook his head. "Even if I knew where to find Fred Little, I have no proof that he's

A to Z 神秘案件

planning a crime."

"But we have to do something!" Ruth Rose said.

"You've already done a lot," Officer Fallon said. "I didn't know that Leona Davis got her bird back. You've given me a good lead. Officer Keene and I really appreciate your help, kids."

He walked them to the door. "Don't worry, we have a few tricks up our sleeves."

"I still think we should do something," Ruth Rose said when they were outside.

"Well…" Josh said. "The circus is leaving tomorrow, and we do have those free tickets Officer Fallon gave us…"

Dink laughed. Together, he and Josh talked Ruth Rose into visiting the circus for a few hours.

They watched a few animal acts and bought popcorn.

Ruth Rose didn't feel like going on any rides, so they decided to go into the clown tent again.

Two clowns dressed as firefighters were running around, bumping into each other while a small cardboard building "burned."

Smoke and fake flames were shooting out of a window. A woman clown was screaming, "Help! Save me!"

Some of the kids in the audience started yelling, "Save her, mister! Up there, save her!"

The firefighter clowns got tangled up in their own hoses, making everyone laugh and yell even louder.

Suddenly a clown dressed like Superman appeared on stilts. He wore a blue shirt under a red cape. Bright yellow suspenders held up the skinny blue pants that hid his stilts.

Superman flapped his cape and snapped his suspenders. Then he marched over to the burning tower and saved the woman. All the kids in the audience yelled and clapped.

Dink noticed that Ruth Rose was hardly even looking. He nudged Josh, and they left.

"I'd like to get me some stilts," Josh said. He walked stiff-legged and snapped invisible suspenders. "Do circuses ever hire kids?"

"Yeah, to feed to the tigers," Dink said, which reminded him of Ruth Rose's Tiger. He looked at her.

"Do you want to come over and finish the Monopoly game?"

She shook her head. "Don't you guys want to solve this mystery?"

"Sure, but what else can we do?" Dink asked. "Officer Fallon said he's gonna look for the people who returned the pets."

"Well, I know how we can help him," Ruth Rose said, her eyes flashing.

金丝雀之谜

"Uh-oh," Josh mumbled.

"Um, Ruth Rose, I don't think Officer Fallon wants any more help," Dink said.

Ruth Rose ignored him. "Are you guys sleeping in the tent again tonight?" she asked.

Dink nodded. "I guess so. Why?"

Ruth Rose grinned mysteriously. "I promise to bring over some cookies if you promise to go somewhere with me."

"Where?" Dink asked. "And why do you have that sneaky look on your face?"

"Wear dark clothes," Ruth Rose said. "We're going to stake out Mrs. Davis's house!"

Chapter 7

"A stakeout?" Josh said.

Ruth Rose nodded.

"Like in the cop movies?" Dink asked.

She nodded again.

"You think Mrs. Davis's house is going to get robbed tonight?" Josh said.

A third nod. "And I plan to be there to see who does it." She grinned. "Will that be enough proof for Officer Fallon?"

"Suppose a burglar does come," Dink said. "What do we do, tie him up?"

"All right!" Josh said. "I'll bring the rope."

Ruth Rose shook her head. "No rope. We just sit and watch. If someone comes, one of us will run to the police station. The other two will stay. If the guy leaves, we follow him."

Dink thought that over. "Follow him where?"

"Wherever he goes, Dink. Maybe he'll lead us to where he stashed the stuff he robbed," Ruth Rose said. "And maybe that's where he's got Tiger."

"Well, I guess it'll work, as long as we just watch the guy," Dink said.

Ruth Rose nodded. "We just wait and watch."

"And eat cookies," Josh added.

Dink and Josh sat in the dark tent, waiting for Ruth Rose. It was almost ten o'clock.

Josh wore camouflage pants and a black T-shirt. Dink had on jeans and a dark gray sweatshirt.

"Where the heck is she?" Josh asked.

Dink peeked out the tent flap. "My folks will kill me if we get caught running around Green Lawn at night."

"Mine would ground me for ten years," Josh said. "Why'd we let her talk us into this?"

Dink heard a noise. "Did you hear something?" he whispered.

Josh peeked out. "Ruth Rose? Is that you?"

"Boo!" Ruth Rose giggled. "I'm right here, Josh."

Dink poked his head out. He couldn't see a thing. "Come on, Ruth Rose, stop fooling around. Where are you hiding?"

"I'm not hiding!" Suddenly Dink could see her. Ruth Rose was sitting about four feet away, right in front of him! She was wearing black jeans and a black jacket. Her hair was covered by a ski cap. She'd even blackened her face. Except for the whites of her eyes, Ruth Rose was practically invisible.

"What's that stuff on your face?" Dink asked.

"Liquid shoe polish." She pulled a bottle out of her backpack. "Here, put some on."

"Do we have to?" Dink said.

"Yes! What happens if the burglar sees your two white faces glowing in the moonlight?"

Dink poured some of the polish into his hand

and smeared it all over his face. "This stuff stinks," he muttered.

Josh did the same. "I feel like Rambo," he said. Dink saw Josh's white teeth gleaming.

"Let's head out," Ruth Rose said, slipping away from the tent.

The boys followed her down Woody Street. Mrs. Davis's house was dark as they crept into her backyard. Dink tried not to think about what they were doing.

Ruth Rose chose their hiding place, a shadowy patch between two thick bushes behind the house.

The moon was almost full, but large clouds kept slipping in front of it. The kids wiggled around, getting comfortable on the lawn.

"Did you bring the cookies?" Josh asked.

"Yes, but let's save them till later," Ruth Rose said. "We might be here for hours."

Josh let out a big sigh. "People who break their promises…"

"She's right, Josh," Dink whispered. "And I don't think we should talk anymore. If the burglar comes, he might hear us and take off."

Five seconds passed.

"One little cookie wouldn't kill you, Ruth Rose."

"Josh, this is a stakeout, not Ellie's Diner."

"Cops eat on stakeouts."

"JOSH! SHHH!"

Dink stretched out on the grass. He watched the back of the house for moving shadows. Nothing moved.

He slapped at a mosquito.

A white cat strolled through the yard.

Dink yawned.

Every few minutes, he checked his watch.

He closed his eyes.

When he opened them again, it was nearly eleven o'clock. Josh was sound asleep, but Dink could see that Ruth Rose's eyes were wide open.

"Are you hungry?" she whispered.

He nodded and shook Josh's shoulder.

Ruth Rose opened her pack. She brought out a bag of cookies, three bananas, and three cartons of apple juice.

They ate in silence, listening and watching for a

burglar to show up.

"Thanks, Ruth Rose," Josh whispered. Then he lay back down and shut his eyes again.

Dink yawned and tried to get comfortable. He wished he'd brought his sleeping bag. It was soft and…suddenly he saw something move in the shadows next to the house.

He shook Josh and put his mouth next to Ruth Rose's ear. "Look," he whispered, pointing.

But whatever he'd seen wasn't moving now.

Dink trained his eyes on the back of the house. He saw only shadows of the trees and bushes.

Then one of the shadows moved.

Dink smelled Josh's cookie breath. "He's here!" Josh whispered. Dink could feel Josh trembling with excitement.

Dink's stomach did a quick plunge. Someone dressed in dark clothes and a baseball cap was creeping behind Mrs. Davis's house. He carried a gym bag and a long pole. The prowler was in the shadows, and Dink couldn't see his face.

The burglar set his bag and the pole on the ground.

Then he checked each first-floor window on the back of the house. Finding them all locked, he walked around the side, out of sight.

"What should we do?" Josh said. "Is he leaving?"

Dink shook his head. "He left his stuff."

"Did anyone recognize his face?" Ruth Rose asked.

Nobody had. Suddenly the dark figure returned. He stood with his back to them, looking up at the house.

Then the prowler turned around. He seemed to be looking directly at Dink.

Dink was glad he'd blackened his face. Suddenly Josh grabbed Dink's arm. "It's the canary guy!"

Ruth Rose let out a gasp.

Fred Little was walking right toward them!

Chapter 8

Dink tried to shrink into the dark space between the bushes. He could feel Josh and Ruth Rose doing the same.

His heart thudded as Fred Little stepped closer. Then he stopped, took off his jacket, and hung it on a tree branch three feet from Dink's nose. He walked back toward the house.

Josh grabbed Dink. "Look, he's wearing yellow suspenders!"

Dink remembered where he'd seen those suspenders. He grinned at Josh. "The Superman clown!"

"And the giraffe clown," Josh whispered back. "I knew I'd seen him before."

They watched as Fred Little opened his gym bag. He pulled out a coil of rope and looped it around his neck.

Then he picked up the long pole he'd brought with him. Only it wasn't a pole.

Fred Little had brought a pair of long stilts. He carefully leaned the stilts against the house and scooted up the foot rests. Now about ten feet tall, he stilt-walked to a spot under a small window on the second floor.

A moment later, Dink watched Fred Little slip through the window. First he was standing there on stilts, and then he was gone, like a snake slithering into a hole.

The stilts remained leaning against the side of the house.

Josh was at Dink's ear. "Should we—"

"Shhh, wait," Ruth Rose whispered.

Suddenly the rope uncoiled from the window. One end dangled to the ground, between the stilts.

"That must be how he's coming down," Ruth Rose said.

"Let's take the rope and stilts," Josh whispered. "He'll be trapped inside!"

"But Mrs. Davis is in there with him," Ruth Rose said. "We have to let him come out, then follow him."

"One of us should run to the police station now," Dink said.

The trouble was, no one wanted to leave the excitement.

Suddenly three things happened at once: The upstairs light blazed on. Dink heard a loud scream. A police whistle blared through the open window.

Dink leaped to his feet, not sure what to do. Mrs. Davis was up there and the burglar was probably in the same room with her!

But which one had let out that scream?

Dink saw a silhouette appear at the window. A second later, Fred Little was climbing down his escape rope. With his feet still above the ground, he dropped.

Suddenly the backyard exploded in color and

noise.

A police cruiser roared across Mrs. Davis's lawn, flashing red, yellow, and blue lights. The backyard looked like a fireworks display.

The siren whooped loudly, shutting out the shrieking of the whistle.

Then the noise stopped as the cruiser doors burst open. Officers Fallon and Keene leaped out.

"Hold it!" Officer Fallon shouted.

Fred Little was still crouched on the ground where he had landed. Dink saw his mouth fall open in panic and surprise.

In seconds, he was wearing handcuffs.

As Officer Keene led the prisoner to the police car, the back door flew open. Mrs. Davis marched out in a white nightgown and floppy slippers. She flip-flopped across the yard toward Fred Little.

Her face was shiny with white cream. Some kind of lacy bonnet covered her hair. And she held a long sword high over her head.

"The nerve of you!" she yelled into Fred Little's terrified face. "Coming right into my bedroom!"

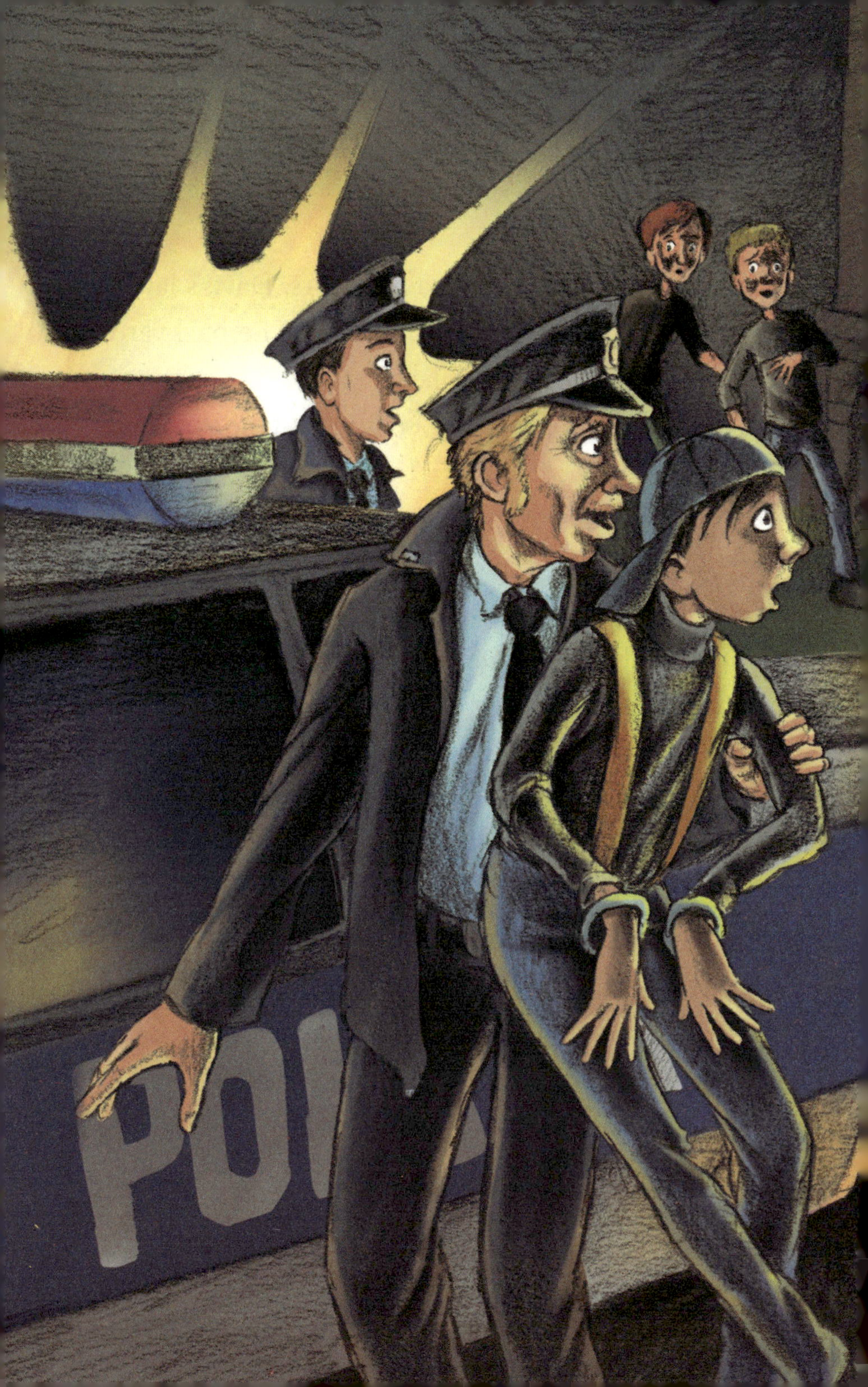

The sword flashed in the cruiser's headlights. Dink thought she was going to use it on the burglar!

"I heard you trying to find my jewelry!" she shouted. "And after I fed you tea and cookies!"

"Come on," Ruth Rose said.

Everyone, but especially Fred Little, was surprised to see three little ninjas crawl out of the bushes.

161

Chapter 9

Ruth Rose stomped up to Fred Little and glared at him. "Where's my Tiger?" she demanded.

Fred Little backed away. "What tiger?"

"Tiger is my cat. Did you steal her? Where is she?"

"I didn't take any cat," he muttered. "I'm allergic to cats."

"What're you kids doing here?" Officer Fallon asked with a frown.

"We thought someone might try to break in tonight," Ruth Rose said, pointing at the prisoner. "We wanted to get proof so you could arrest him."

"This is Fred Little," Josh said. "The guy who returned Mrs. Davis's canary. He's also a clown in the circus."

"And he's probably the one who robbed Dr. Pardue's house and the Gwynns', too," Dink added.

"It certainly looks that way," Officer Fallon said. He gave instructions to Officer Keene, who locked Fred Little in the cruiser and drove away.

Officer Fallon looked sternly at Dink. "We'll talk tomorrow," he said. "You kids better skedaddle home and get some sleep."

"Fiddlesticks!" Mrs. Davis said. "These children won't perish if they stay up a little longer. And I won't sleep a wink! Come inside for cookies and cocoa, all of you."

Officer Fallon just smiled and shook his head as they followed Mrs. Davis into her kitchen. Dink noticed Mozart's cage sitting on the counter.

Mrs. Davis put water on to boil and took mugs from a cupboard. Then she pulled the cover off the birdcage. Mozart twittered and blinked his tiny black eyes.

A to Z 神秘案件

"You've certainly put everyone through a lot of trouble," she told her canary.

"Actually, Leona, your canary helped us to solve a string of burglaries," Officer Fallon said. "I did some snooping and found out a lot about Fred Little and his girlfriend. They've been traveling with the circus, and robbing houses in the towns they visit, for quite some time. And they always do it the same way. First they steal pets. Then they return the pets to get a peek inside the houses. Later, they rob the same houses."

Mrs. Davis shook her head. "You should have seen that creepy man's face when I turned on the light. But how did he know I left my upstairs bathroom window open?"

"He probably saw that it was open when he took your canary," Officer Fallon said.

"Or maybe he left it open," Dink said. "He might have snuck upstairs when he used the bathroom."

"You could be right, Dink," Officer Fallon said. "On stilts, he could get into upstairs windows that most people leave unlocked. In the robbery business, he's known as a second-story man."

"After tonight," Mrs. Davis said, "that window will be locked!"

"How did you know that Fred Little would try to break in tonight?" Dink asked.

"We were parked right around the corner," Officer Fallon continued. "We figured the burglary had to be tonight or never, since the circus leaves town tomorrow."

Suddenly there was a knock at the door. Officer Fallon stood up and stretched. "That'll be Officer Keene back with the car. We'll drive you kids home now. I hope we didn't wreck your yard, Leona."

"Oh, pooh. You saved my jewelry and caught a pair of criminals," she said. "Besides, I know three children who might like to earn some money raking and planting grass seed."

Officer Fallon laughed. "You could have caught Fred Little all by yourself. Where'd that sword come from, Leona?"

"My husband brought it back from one of our trips," she said, smiling. "It's been under my bed for years, in case I ever needed it."

"Did you see that guy's face?" Josh asked. "I think he was glad to go to jail!"

Officer Fallon and Officer Keene dropped the kids off at Dink's house. "Good night, kids," Officer Fallon said. "No more sneaking around, okay?"

The kids promised they'd go right to bed and watched the cruiser drive away.

"I wonder if Fred Little was telling the truth about Tiger," Ruth Rose said. "All the pets got returned except mine."

"Tomorrow we'll help you search, right, Josh?" Dink said.

"Right," Josh said. "We'll ring every doorbell in Green Lawn if we have to."

Ruth Rose nodded, looking sad. "Thanks, guys."

The boys said good night to Ruth Rose, then walked around back and crawled into their tent.

Josh giggled in the dark. "Did you see Mrs. Davis come flying out her door with all that goop on her face? I thought she was a ghost!"

Dink grinned. "Yeah, and old Fred Little came

shooting out the window like a rocket. I bet he burned his hands sliding down that rope."

Dink rolled over and closed his eyes.

Thirty seconds later, Ruth Rose burst through the tent flap. She shined a flashlight into Dink's face.

"GUYS, WAKE UP!" she yelled.

Josh bolted straight up. "Geez, Ruth Rose, my heart can't take any more surprises tonight."

"What's wrong?" Dink asked, blinking.

"TIGER CAME HOME!" Ruth Rose said, flopping down next to Dink's feet. "She was on my bed when

I snuck upstairs. When I went to pick her up, she hopped down and crawled under the bed."

Ruth Rose grinned. "And guess what I found under there with her?"

"A sword?" Dink guessed.

"Nope!"

"A burglar?" Josh asked, blinking into the flashlight.

"No! I found three kittens. I'M A GRAND-MOTHER!"

Text copyright © 1998 by Ron Roy
Cover art copyright © 2015 by Stephen Gilpin
Interior illustrations copyright © 1998 by John Steven Gurney
All rights reserved. Published in the United States by Random House Children's Books,
a division of Random House LLC, a Penguin Random House Company, New York.
Originally published in paperback by Random House Children's Books, New York, in 1998.

本书中英双语版由中南博集天卷文化传媒有限公司与企鹅兰登（北京）文化发展有限公司合作出版。

"企鹅"及其相关标识是企鹅兰登已经注册或尚未注册的商标。
未经允许，不得擅用。
封底凡无企鹅防伪标识者均属未经授权之非法版本。

©中南博集天卷文化传媒有限公司。本书版权受法律保护。未经权利人许可，任何人不得以任何方式使用本书包括正文、插图、封面、版式等任何部分内容，违者将受到法律制裁。

著作权合同登记号：字18-2023-258

图书在版编目（CIP）数据

金丝雀之谜：汉英对照／（美）罗恩·罗伊著；
（美）约翰·史蒂文·格尼绘；高琼译. -- 长沙：湖南
少年儿童出版社，2024.10. --（A to Z神秘案件）.
ISBN 978-7-5562-7817-6

Ⅰ．H319.4

中国国家版本馆CIP数据核字第2024C1P489号

A TO Z SHENMI ANJIAN JINSIQUE ZHI MI

A to Z神秘案件 金丝雀之谜

［美］罗恩·罗伊 著　　［美］约翰·史蒂文·格尼 绘　　高琼 译

责任编辑：唐 凌　李 炜	策划出品：李 炜　张苗苗　文赛峰
策划编辑：文赛峰	特约编辑：张晓璐
营销编辑：付 佳　杨 朔　周晓茜	封面设计：霍雨佳
版权支持：王媛媛	版式设计：马睿君
插图上色：河北传图文化	内文排版：马睿君

出 版 人：刘星保
出　　版：湖南少年儿童出版社
地　　址：湖南省长沙市晚报大道89号
邮　　编：410016
电　　话：0731-82196320
常年法律顾问：湖南崇民律师事务所　柳成柱律师
经　　销：新华书店
开　　本：875 mm×1230 mm　1/32　　印　　刷：三河市中晟雅豪印务有限公司
字　　数：94千字　　　　　　　　　　　印　　张：5.375
版　　次：2024年10月第1版　　　　　　印　　次：2024年10月第1次印刷
书　　号：ISBN 978-7-5562-7817-6　　　定　　价：280.00元（全10册）

若有质量问题，请致电质量监督电话：010-59096394　团购电话：010-59320018